Time and Tide

The Transformation of Bear River, Nova Scotia

Stephen J. Hornsby

Northeast Folklore Vol. 31: 1996

NORTHEAST FOLKLORE

Volume XXXI   1996

Published annually by The Maine Folklife Center,
5773 South Stevens Hall
University of Maine
Orono, Maine 04469-5773

Edward D. Ives, Editor

Pauleena M. MacDougall, Managing Editor

Designed by Michael Mardosa, University of Maine Department of Public Affairs
Printed by University of Maine Printing Services
Orono, Maine, 1996

The Maine Folklife Center is a non-profit organization devoted to the collection, preservation, study and publication of the songs, legends, tales and other traditions of New England and the Atlantic Provinces of Canada. Regular annual membership is $25.00 per year. All members receive the Maine Folklife Center Newsletter as it appears and a subscription to *Northeast Folklore,* as well as a ten percent discount on tapes, books and videos as a privilege of membership.

Northeast Folklore is an annual publication issued by the Maine Folklife Center, formerly the Northeast Folklore Society. Each year we hope to publish a single fresh collection of regional material or a comparative study, but we do not rule out the possibility of making a single volume out of several shorter collections or studies. Authors are invited to submit manuscripts for consideration to The Editor, *Northeast Folklore,* South Stevens Hall, University of Maine, Orono, Maine 04469.

ISBN 0-943197-23-6

Front Cover: Detail, Chapter 1, Plate 34.

Frontispiece: Aerial view of Bear River looking down river towards Annapolis Basin, Digby Gut, and the Bay of Fundy, c.1960. (D.B. Field, Weymouth, NS)

For Edgar McKay

Whose lifelong interest in
Bear River made this book possible

Contents

Preface

THE CONTOURS of modernization in Canada have been thrown into increasingly sharp relief in recent years. Much is now known about the rise of the Canadian nation-state, industrialization, urbanization, and the "limited identities" of class, race, and gender.[1] Yet much less is known about the impact of modernization on the Canadian countryside.[2] Most historical studies of rural Canada have focused on the great themes of European immigration, settlement, and economic development in the seventeenth, eighteenth, and nineteenth centuries. Few studies have looked at the great changes that affected the Canadian countryside in the early twentieth century.[3] New communication and transportation technologies, agricultural mechanization, changing market demand, increasing intervention by the state, influence of urban fashion, and lure of better paying jobs in cities all combined to remake rural life. In the first fifty years of the twentieth century, a new Canadian countryside was born.

By looking at the impact of modernization on one small community in southwestern Nova Scotia, *Time and Tide* tells something of this story. Using mainly oral testimony and historic photographs, this book explores the dramatic economic and social changes that affected Bear River in the early twentieth century. Among these changes were the collapse of the traditional economies of farming, lumbering, shipbuilding, and shipping that dominated Bear River in the early 1900s, the failure to replace them with new industries such as pulp and paper milling, and the growing importance of tourism and the state in maintaining the community in the 1930s, 1940s, and 1950s. While these economic changes were occurring, the community was becoming increasingly integrated into the regional and national space. Roads, automobiles, radios, telephones, welfare programs, and circulation of money all helped tie Bear River into the larger Canadian nation-state. Although the details and circumstances of these changes are unique to Bear River, the general story has considerable relevance for our understanding of the impact of modernization on many other parts of rural Canada.

The study is based largely on material collected by Professor Edgar McKay in the mid-1950s. Born in Boston in 1903, Ed McKay was sent by his mother to Bear River in 1912 to stay with his grandparents and receive a grade-school education. After six years at school, Ed left Bear River and went back to the "Boston States," staying first with an uncle in Melrose,

Opposite: Ship being towed by a motor launch through the old drawbridge in the center of Bear River, c. 1912. The ship was on its way to the Tom Rice shipyard for repairs. The launch, which belonged to the local bank manager, was used for towing jobs such as this, as well as for pleasure trips.

Massachusetts, and then with another uncle in Winslow, Maine, where he worked on the farm. A few years later, he returned to school and completed his high school education. After obtaining a degree at Colby College, Maine, and teaching school for a spell in Winslow, Ed joined the faculty at the University of Maine in 1947, where he stayed until retiring in 1973. Throughout these years, Ed maintained his mother's residence in Bear River, visiting there every summer.

In the early 1950s, Ed McKay met Dr. Alexander Leighton, Professor of Psychiatry and Professor of Sociology and Social Anthropology at Cornell University, then engaged in research in social psychiatry in southwestern Nova Scotia.[4] Funded by the Rockefeller Foundation of New York and part of a much larger American social science project to understand the impact of modernization on "traditional" societies around the world, Leighton's massive ten-year Stirling County Study looked at the relationship between psychiatric disorder and sociocultural environment. As part of Bear River lay within the research area of Stirling County (the fictional name for Digby County), Leighton encouraged Ed McKay to collect material on the community. Although not trained in social psychiatry, Ed was able to gather information on the "sociocultural environment." As a member of the Bear River community, Ed had a unique entrée into the life of the town. Yet his professional training in sociology and his twenty-year association with Leighton's research team also allowed him to stand apart from the community and view it from outside. With his "expert knowledge" and connections to Leighton, Ed was as much a part of the modernization process in Bear River as the new industrial technologies and welfare programs of the Canadian nation-state.

Like many social scientists studying modernization in the 1950s, Leighton employed a conceptual framework in his Stirling county study that owed much to the influential ideas of Ferdinand Tönnies. Tönnies argued that modernization involved a transition from traditional, "folk-type" communities (*Gemeinschaft*) to modern, industrial societies (*Gesellschaft*). In this transition, household production based on agriculture was replaced by trade and industry, folkways and custom by state legislation and laws of contract, and tradition by utilitarian values. With "the primary economic relationship to the natural world, the informal daily work practices, the widespread face-to-face communication, and the small village and traditional family way of life," the rural communities of southwest Nova Scotia, according to Leighton, closely approximated Tönnies's model of *Gemeinschaft*.[5] Such a model undoubtedly influenced Ed McKay's thinking about Bear River and is reflected in his unpublished notes. Nevertheless, much of the material that he collected was of an economic, rather than social or cultural, nature. Ed sought to trace the collapse of the old wood, wind, and sail economy and its replacement by tourism and government welfare. He scoured through local newspapers, collected a variety of information about the economic history of the community, and interviewed many people over the age of fifty. Most of the interviewees were men, and many had worked in farming, lumbering, sawmilling, shipping, or shipbuilding, but he gathered very little information from or about women.

Among the documents that Ed McKay collected was a remarkable set of views of Bear River taken by local storekeeper and photographer Ralph Harris in the early 1900s. Given permission by Harris, Ed selected about fifty images from hundreds of glass negatives in the studio. Soon after the prints were made and before the negatives could be acquired by the Provincial Archives of Nova Scotia, the studio burnt down, with the total loss of the glass plates. The photographs that survive today include the images reproduced in this book, plus a few others (in the form of postcards) in the Provincial Archives, the Nova Scotia Museum, and the Bear River Historical Society. Some of these photographs have been previously published in a local history, *Heritage Remembered: The Story of Bear River.*[6] Besides intending to use the photographs to illustrate his study of Bear River, Ed employed them in the interviews to prompt conversation and elicit information. He was thus able to identify the time, place, and people depicted in many of the scenes.

Ralph Harris was a professional photographer, who did "all outside work including photos of dwellings, groups, etc."[7] He appears to have worked only in Bear River and the surrounding area of Lake Joli, Smiths Cove, Annapolis Basin, Digby, and Annapolis Royal.[8] All the photographs McKay selected date from 1905 to 1921, a period coinciding with the end of the old wood, wind, and sail economy. Harris used some of the photographs to make postcards, which he then sold in his store to visiting tourists. Although these postcards frequently depicted the waning lumber and sailing trades, the cards themselves were part of the emerging tourist industry that was gradually replacing the old staple industries in Nova Scotia. While chronicling the passing of hand logging and the sailing ship, Harris was also helping shape the future of Bear River as a tourist resort.

Much of the professional photography of Nova Scotia in the 1910s and 1920s served the tourist industry and frequently portrayed the countryside in a sentimental and pastoral way. This was especially true of photographers depicting the Annapolis Valley, the "Land of Evangeline," for the publicists of the Dominion Atlantic Railway.[9] Acadian maids standing in front of apple trees loaded with blossom were standard shots. Yet the photographs taken by Harris are striking for their straightforward and honest depiction of the working landscapes of Bear River. Of course, Ed McKay may have filtered out sentimental views, but the chance survival of other images in public collections suggests that McKay's selection accurately represents Harris's *oeuvre.* Unlike photographers in the Annapolis Valley, Harris lacked a powerful patron, such as the Dominion Atlantic, to dictate the type of photograph taken, and he was thus free to photograph what he liked. The photographs include landscapes, ranging from panoramic views of Bear River and Lake Joli to streetscapes, riverscapes, and pictures of individual buildings; depictions of social life, particularly town carnivals and parades; and portraits of work in the fields, woods, mills, and shipyards. The photographs were taken at all seasons, although pastoral views of Bear River at blossom time were rare, perhaps indicating Harris's aversion to the picturesque.

The honest, unsentimental vision revealed in the photographs reflected much about Harris. The son of a local farmer, Harris spent his life in Bear River and knew the area intimately. His major recreations were trout fishing and deer hunting in "the back country," and he boasted of having fished most of the best waters in western Nova Scotia "when there was real fishing." The photographs of Bear River taken from many different viewpoints and in all seasons, as well as the depictions of lumbering in the back woods reveal this familiarity. A lifelong and fairly active member of the Baptist Church, a consistent supporter of the Conservative Party, and the owner of his own business, Harris believed in the virtues of self-reliance and hard work. In the mid-1950s, Ed McKay characterized him as one of Bear River's "rugged individualists," vehemently opposed to government welfare. "To [Harris] there is something definitely immoral in having a government that compels him to pay higher taxes 'to support a lot of lazy bums' and whom he regards as better able to work than he is."[10] The photographs of farm laborers and lumberers reflect this belief in the value of hard work, although there is little or no attempt to depict labor in a heroic way. Harris had a reputation for strong opinions and blunt speaking, and this single-mindedness and directness is shown in several photographs depicting farm labor, particularly those of farmers picking strawberries, tapping maple trees, and loading turnips. These are concentrated, honest portraits, with no hint of artifice or the picturesque. Such photographs stand out from the general run-of-the-mill work done by many of his contemporaries elsewhere in Nova Scotia. In their documentary realism and choice of subject, they have much in common with the photographs of shipping and lumbering taken about the same time by Charles Pratsch in Aberdeen, Washington State.[11] Harris's photographs are among the finest depictions of a community in the Canadian Maritimes that we have and serve as a powerful memorial to a vanished way of life.

Unfortunately, Ed McKay was never able to publish these photographs. Amid busy teaching and administrative responsibilities at the University of Maine (Ed was co-founder with Alice Stewart of the Canadian-American Center in 1967), he never found time to work up his study. A five-page summary entitled "Some Brief Notes on the Economic History of Bear River" gives some idea of the book that might have been written. The type-written sheets and photographs remained crammed in an old steel typewriter box until 1992 when he contacted me. He had just heard about my book on Cape Breton and thought I might be interested in some material he had collected on Nova Scotia. I well remember going over to his apartment, talking about Cape Breton and trout fishing, and then being shown a grey steel box. Un-clipping the lid, I realized I had stumbled on a treasure trove. The photographs made the most immediate impact, revealing a world that was now completely lost. Only later, while reading through the interviews, did I realize that Ed had recorded a wealth of information about farming, lumbering, and shipbuilding that would have otherwise disappeared. In addition to these records, Ed had collected local newspapers, and helped get the voluminous records of Clarke Brothers, the leading lumber merchants in Bear River, deposited in the Public Archives of Nova Scotia. Taken together, the interviews, photographs, newspapers, and archival records provided enough material to work up into a small book.

Although respectful of the ideas contained in Ed McKay's unpublished notes about Bear River, I have attempted to bring a geographer's perspective to bear on the material as well as to introduce some of the ideas about modernization put forward by sociologist Anthony Giddens. Taking his cue from geographers, Giddens argues that modernization involved significant changes in the spatial and temporal framework of life and work. As the modern nation-state emerged, economic and political systems were increasingly stretched over time and space, linking together previously isolated places. Bundles of social and economic relationships that were once embedded in local places have been replaced by ties that stretch across nations and, even, around the world. Such a change, it seems to me, characterized early twentieth-century Bear River.

In writing *Time and Tide,* I have incurred many debts. Most especially, I could not have written it without the cooperation of Ed McKay. Besides providing much of the primary material, he commented upon the text, suggested the title, and gave great encouragement. In many ways, the book is very much his creation. His late wife, Ruth, who helped Ed collect material and typed up the extensive field notes, was also extremely supportive. Ed's daughter, Jean Timpa, generously read the manuscript and suggested some changes. Various drafts have benefitted from comments by Robert Babcock, David Demeritt, Cole Harris, Larry McCann, and Graeme Wynn. Publication of the book owes much to Edward "Sandy" Ives, who suggested that it should appear in *Northeast Folklore,* and to Pauleena MacDougall, who not only helped with the editing but saw the book through the press. The staffs of the Public Archives of Nova Scotia and the library of Mount Allison University have been helpful in providing materials. Professor Alexander Leighton kindly gave permission for the reproduction of photographs from the Stirling County Study held in the Public Archives of Nova Scotia. Ray Harris, Department of Geography, University of Edinburgh, drew the maps. A Canadian Studies Research Grant generously provided by the Canadian Embassy, Washington DC helped support the research.

Copies of the notes and interviews done by Edgar McKay and the photographs taken by Ralph Harris have been deposited in the Maine Folklife Center, University of Maine, and in the Public Archives of Nova Scotia. Unless otherwise credited, all photographs in the text are from the Ralph Harris Collection.

Introduction

IN THE late nineteenth and early twentieth centuries, the pattern of settlement and economy that had emerged in Canada since the seventeenth century was transformed. The early pattern of scattered settlement, long-distance staple trades, and pockets of semi-subsistence agriculture was over-ridden by an emerging nation-state, urban-industrial development, and modern communications and transportation.[1] Disparate settlements that had been individually tied into a North Atlantic commercial world, centered first on France and then on Great Britain, were gradually knit together into a continental economy focused on Central Canada. At the same time, the local worlds of outport, lumber camp, fur post, farm, and village, where much life and work depended on face-to-face interaction, were gradually enveloped by the faceless nation-state and the economic and social influences of burgeoning industrial cities. Whereas the political and economic systems of colonial Canada had only limited reach over time and space, those of modern Canada became increasingly stretched, binding places together. Modernization had dramatically increased what Anthony Giddens has called "time-space distanciation."[2]

The binding of the Maritime provinces into the new political and economic order of the Canadian nation-state involved a massive reorientation away from Great Britain and the Atlantic world towards Central Canada and the continent. The process began with Confederation in 1867 and the National Policy of 1879.[3] Political union replaced the old colonial tie to London with a federal link to Ottawa. The National Policy of protective tariffs and trans-continental railways promised to replace the region's staple trades that sent fish and lumber by sea to markets around the North Atlantic with new industries that would send manufactured goods by rail to markets in Central and Western Canada. The old economy of wood, wind, and sail would be replaced by a new one of iron, coal, and rail. By the 1880s, this promise of an industrial future appeared fulfilled. Many merchants in the Maritimes had divested themselves of the old staple trades and were investing in new industries.[4] Yet by the early twentieth century, a weak resource base, distance from national markets, high transportation costs, and corporate consolidation in Central Canada had undermined much of this early industrialization.[5] As the region experienced economic difficulties in the 1920s and 1930s, the Maritimes increasingly found itself a ward of the federal state. Yet, paradoxically, economic decline helped

Opposite: Lake Joli clothespin factory c.1915. There were three clothespin machines in this part of the mill, each with a daily capacity of 75 boxes of finished pins. These pins were the old-fashioned "dolly" common round clothespins. Local female labor was hired to work in the factory. The persons are from left to right in front: Alfred Cashman, Florence Early, Vada Wambolt, and Gladys Porter; in back: Fred Porter, Alice Banks, and Boyd Rice (foreman).

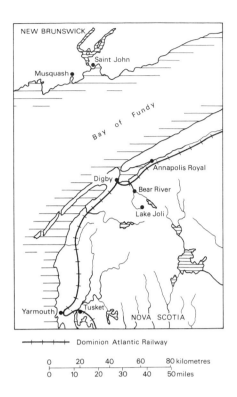

Fig. 1. *Location of Bear River, Nova Scotia*

preserve towns and countryside from industrial development, making them attractive to middle class tourists from industrial cities in Central Canada and New England. Federal transfer payments and tourists helped integrate the region into the Canadian and continental economies.

Underlying these political and economic shifts were new transport and communication technologies that increasingly opened up the Maritimes to external influences. The completion of the Intercolonial Railway in 1876 and the spread of the railway net throughout the region linked towns to regional metropolises and to Central and Western Canada.[6] Meanwhile, steamboat services along the coast and across the Gulf of Maine facilitated economic and social ties to New England. In the early twentieth century, trunk roads linked Maine to New Brunswick and the other Maritime provinces. Such transportation links brought in manufactured goods and tourists and took out raw materials and emigrants. The spread of the national mail service (the post office was often the only visible federal presence in many small towns), telephones, and radios also allowed rapid communication across the country and with the United States. Efficient political and economic control over the region from outside was now possible, and modern urban popular culture, manifest in ways of speech, dress, and entertainment, was increasingly within reach for people living in the Maritimes. Taken together, these political, economic, cultural, and technological processes had created a new spatial grid, dramatically reordering lives and work in the region.

Among many places in Maritime Canada affected by these processes of modernization was the small, rural community of Bear River, Nova Scotia. Situated four miles inland from Annapolis Basin and bisected by the Digby/Annapolis county line, Bear River was a thriving place in the last quarter of the nineteenth century (Figure 1). With a peak population of 2,000 in 1881, the inhabitants of Bear River made a living from semi-subsistence farming, lumbering, small-scale manufacturing, shipbuilding, and shipping, as well as employment in the "Boston States." Virtually all the farms, sawmills, retail businesses, and ships were owned locally, and Bear River people did much of their business with resident merchants. The export of agricultural produce across the Bay of Fundy to Saint John and of lumber down the eastern seaboard to Boston, New York, and the Caribbean tied Bear River into an extensive maritime spatial economy. Links with the rest of Canada, however, were limited. The Dominion Atlantic Railway, which could have provided landward connections, by-passed the town. Many people had little direct experience of the world beyond southwest Nova Scotia and the Saint John-Boston axis, and most spent their day-to-day lives within a fairly circumscribed territory. Although the inhabitants of Bear River lived under provincial law, filled out federal censuses, used the federal post office, and entered import and export cargoes in the town's customs house, government did not intrude into the everyday life of most people. Because of the prevailing ideology of *laissez-faire* and dominance of Protestantism, most people believed that individual hard work and self-reliance would bring material advancement.

By the early 1950s, the same could not be said. The traditional economy had collapsed; outside firms controlled the few remaining important businesses. The population had fallen by a third, and many of those who remained depended on earnings from tourists, government employment, and federal pensions and welfare. From being a place almost completely dependent on its own local economy, Bear River had become reliant on tourists "from away" and a distant government. Paved roads, automobiles, mail-order catalogues, radios, and telephones tied the town to the rest of Canada. Outside political and economic forces had dramatically reshaped Bear River's identity. The once intimate connection between people and place had loosened, leaving the inhabitants of Bear River vulnerable to powerful external influences over which they had little or no control.

This book charts this transformation, beginning with the settlement, economy, and society of Bear River in the opening decades of the twentieth century and then considering the changes that took place between 1890 and 1950. A final section examines the broader processes that lay behind the modernization of Bear River and much of the rest of the rural Maritimes.

1

Bear River Country, 1890–1920

EUROPEAN settlement in Bear River began after the end of the American War of Independence, when Hessian and Waldeck troops took land grants in the area.[1] Many of these German settlers soon moved on, leaving only a few place names to mark their brief stay. A mix of New Englanders and Loyalists, who trickled into the Bear River Valley from other parts of Nova Scotia in the late 1780s, and English settlers, mostly from Yorkshire, who arrived in the 1830s, occupied the vacant land. The few Micmacs in the area lived on a reservation at the back of town.

The European settlers who moved into the Bear River Valley found little good agricultural land. Unlike the broad Annapolis Valley to the northeast, there was little intervale or valley bottom land in Bear River and most farms were laid out on the sides of steep hills. To the north of town, well-drained loamy soils of fair agricultural capability had developed on the underlying shales, slates, and quartzite, but to the south only thin, acidic soils of no agricultural potential covered the granite bedrock. "These hillsides were never meant for farming" commented Harold Davis, a farmer on the Annapolis side of Bear River, "they're only fit for moose and bear and wildcats and Indians."[2] Scattered farms emerged along the valley, the road to Lansdowne, and the Hessian line to Bear River East and Clementsvale (Figure 2). After the best land had been taken, settlement pushed on to the granite hills in the back country, creating the straggling communities of Morganville and Greenland. Tributaries of Bear River, however, provided good water-power sites and the tide reached up much of the river. At the head of the tide, accessible to ocean-going vessels, and close to the best water-power sites, a small, nucleated service center, known as "The Bridge," grew up. It was the focus of the economic and social life of the valley and surrounding area.

By the end of the nineteenth century, "The Bridge" or village of Bear River was well established. The compact central business district focused on the river, the main means of communication with the outside world. Wharves and warehouses lined the waterfront, and retail stores competed for space along Main Street (Plates 1–2). Along some parts of the street, buildings had been built on piles over the river, while in other parts subdivision of lots had produced an almost continuous street frontage. Main Street was the most "urban" looking part of town (Plate 3). As competition for space lessened away from the river, businesses that still needed a central location but could not pay the highest rents, such as the Grand Central

Opposite: Byron Harris farm, near Bear River, c.1920. Ira Harris hilling potatoes using a one-horse rig with Lovett Apt holding the hiller. The crop shown here amounted to over 150 bushels of potatoes, an unusually large one for the Bear River area.

19

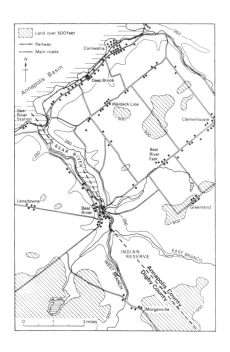

Fig. 2. Bear River area (Based on National Topographic Series, Digby, NS, 1950)

House and artisans' workshops, were found. On the west side of town, several small industries that needed waterpower—tanneries, blacksmiths shops, and a carding mill—had located along Wade Brook. On the hillsides overlooking the river were churches, cemeteries, a school, and a temperance hall. Many of the residences in town were also found above the floodplain, some cut into the hillsides to gain level ground (Plate 4).

After more than a century of growth, Bear River was a relatively prosperous settlement with a diversified economy. Most people made a living from either semi-subsistence farming, lumbering, sawmilling, small-scale manufacturing, shipbuilding, or shipping. Local people owned and controlled Bear River's farms, woods, mills, workshops, shipyards, and stores, and they looked seaward to sell their products. Lumber and agricultural produce were shipped by water to markets around the North Atlantic. With few landward economic ties, Bear River was essentially an export enclave. Although some inhabitants "worked away," particularly in the "Boston States," and Bear River's ship captains and crew could be found from Saint John to Havana, most people spent their daily lives close to town. This combination of an export enclave and persistent localism was characteristic of much of Maritime Canada in the nineteenth and early twentieth centuries.[3]

Farming

The farms in Bear River were relatively small and unspecialized, serving mainly local needs. Of 337 farms listed in the 1891 census, 142 (42 percent) were small-holdings of less than 11 acres. Situated in the back country, they belonged to laborers who worked in the woods and local sawmills. A further 147 farms (44 percent) were between 11 and 200 acres; the remaining 48 farms (15 percent) were more than 200 acres. Much of the land on these farms was in woodlot, while the cleared or "improved" area was mostly in rough pasture or grass.[4] Nevertheless, the steep slopes and well-drained soils of the Bear River Valley were not good hay land, a critical limitation on livestock raising (Plate 5).

"Bear River never grew any great amount of hay," recalled Harold Davis, although demand for hay from farmers, as well as from the local timber industry, was considerable (Plate 6). Natural meadows, deep in the backwoods, were cut. According to Davis, all the meadow lands in the woods "were hayed in the old days...I can remember when they used to cut the Parker Meadow at Chub Brook, and there was the Joe Snell Meadow, the Chisholm Meadow, and up in the Big Lake Country [Mulgrave Lake], there was Flanders Meadow and...Joshua Peck used to hay at Annie Morehouse Lake and haul the hay to Bear River." Such names indicated the family who owned and cut the area. Cutting of meadows in the back woods was usually done in late summer after the home farm "had been cut." The hay was mowed with a hand scythe, raked with a hand-rake, and stacked with pitch fork around a hay pole on the meadow, sometimes on a platform above the expected high water mark. The hay makers usually camped at these woodland meadows for a week or so, either in a tent, camp, or brush "lean-to." In the winter, after the roads and swamps were well frozen, an ox-team went back to the meadow for the hay. As the meadows were from ten to fifteen miles from Bear River, this usually involved an overnight trip in subfreezing weather. The teams "left Bear River one day, and they had to camp out over night, and take all next day to get back to town."[5]

Farmers and lumberers also imported hay from Digby and Saint John. "Herb" Hazelton, odd job man, "rough carpenter," and former cook on the steamer *Bear River*, recalled "We always had a deck load of hay.... Sometimes we made special trips to Digby for hay."[6] John Morine, fireman on the *Bear River*, recollected "that large quantities of hay and feed were always brought into Bear River by Clarke Brothers for their lumber operations. A consistent pattern was a carload of hay and grain on each trip, sometimes three carloads—including flour and feed."[7]

Given limited hay land, the expense of importing hay, and the difficulty of competing with western beef and grain in urban markets, most farmers raised only food for their families and small surpluses for sale in niche markets.[8] They kept one or two beef cattle, a "family cow" for butter and milk, a few sheep and hens, and a pig for winter slaughter. Farmers used oxen for ploughing (particularly suitable for Bear River's hilly terrain), as well as for hauling timber out of the woods. The few farmers that owned a horse or a team were looked upon as "wealthy" and "progressive."[9] Although many farmers grew grain (wheat, buckwheat, barley, oats), flour was imported in quantity from the United States and Ontario. They also raised roots (potatoes, turnips, beets), vegetables (peas, beans, carrots, onions, corn),[10] and fruit (Plate 7). Potatoes and vegetables were for family consumption, while turnips and mangle beets were ground in a "cutter" and then fed to cattle. Many of the more "progressive" farmers fed their milking cows mangles instead of turnips, as "turnips gave the milk a strong flavour."[11]

Harold Davis's farm was typical of the better operations. Located on the east side of Bear River, the farm comprised approximately seventy acres, including fields, pasture, and woodlot. Although it had a hilly situation, it was regarded as a "good farm" in the early years of the century. Davis always had a yoke of oxen on his farm, usually a horse, several milk cows and young cattle; he also raised vegetables and fruit for local markets and was thought by people to make a "rather good living."[12]

The main agricultural exports from Bear River were butter and eggs for the Saint John market and fruit for regional and overseas markets. As Figure 3 shows, Clarke Brothers, the leading merchants in Bear River in the early twentieth century, collected butter, eggs, soft fruits, vegetables, roots, and meat. In 1910, they bought $3,180 of butter and eggs, 55 percent of their total grocery purchases. Much of this produce was shipped to Saint John. The perishable nature of butter, eggs, soft fruits, and vegetables kept out produce from farmers in Québec and Ontario and allowed local farmers to compete in the Saint John market.[13]

The main fruit exports were cherries and apples, cherries being a local specialty. In the first decades of the century, Bear River put on a cherry festival and a "Cherry Sunday" each year. "Cherry Sunday" was usually a Sunday around the 20th of July when hundreds of visitors came into town

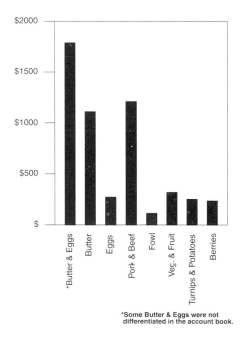

Fig. 3. Produce purchased by Clarke Brothers from local farmers, 1910. (Clarke Papers MG 3/3507 Journal Public Archives of Nova Scotia)

to "buy" trees or purchase boxes of cherries. Owners of cherry orchards "rented" or "sold" trees to parties for between .50¢ and $3.00 a tree. The purchaser then took his family "to pick the tree clean" (Plate 8). Some farms had from a dozen to as many as twenty cherry trees and marketed over a thousand boxes of cherries each.[14] Cherries also were shipped to Saint John, Halifax, and Boston. The $2-3,000 return on sales provided the hundred or more families who sent cherries to market with "a very convenient source of pin money for the summer months."[15]

Although apple growing was less prominent than in the towns of the neighboring Annapolis Valley,[16] Bear River in good years exported 10,000 to 12,000 barrels of apples to Annapolis Royal or Saint John for consignment to the English market. The usual varieties of apples for export were Northern Spy, Baldwin, and Greening, but nearly every farm also had Gravenstein, Sweet Bough, Red Astrakhan, King, Russet, Blenheim Pippin, Ribston Pippin, and many others practically unheard of today (Plate 9). A few farms also produced soft fruits, such as strawberries, and maple syrup for sale (Plates 10–11).

Farmers and merchants in Bear River handled the agricultural export trade. A few farmers sent wagon loads of roots to Bear River Station on the Dominion Atlantic for consignment to agents in Yarmouth, who then shipped them to Boston. Others took the steamer from Bear River to Saint John to sell produce. John Morine remembered "People [would] take their own things across to sell—like Charles Lent in Deep Brook. He used to take meat, vegetables and fruit and he'd have a stall in the big Saint John market. He'd sell his stuff and return with us in three days and he'd make a pretty good thing out of the trip." For those who could not take the boat, Morine acted as middleman: "Sometimes people from Deep Brook would give me butter and eggs and vegetables at the Victoria Bridges to sell for them in Saint John; sometimes I'd buy things from folks in town to sell myself, or I'd buy eggs from A.B. Marshall [Bear River merchant]—he always had plenty of eggs that people brought in for pay—and I'd pay the regular freight charges...the same as anyone else had to. I made a little money selling things and doing business for folks that way, sometimes more than my wages."[17]

More commonly, farmers brought their produce to the stores of town merchants and received cash, credit, or goods in return (Plate 12).[18] At least in the early years of the century, a barter economy with long credit still operated in Bear River. In 1901, A.B. Marshall, one of the leading merchants in Bear River at that time, advertised "HIGH GRADE GROCERIES...and Standard Dry Goods—FLOUR..., Dried Pollock and CODFISH, Choice Porto Rico MOLASSES..." with "Cordwood, Piling, Butter and Eggs wanted in exchange."[19] After collecting cargoes of butter, eggs, fruit, vegetables, and roots, as well as lumber, the town's merchants then sent them to Saint John or Boston (Plate 13).[20] These export shipments paid for imported cargoes of flour and dry goods. Al Marshall bought almost entirely "through John G. Hall in Boston, especially flour [and] sent cordwood and piling to pay for it...we settled the balance after the trip in gold coins."[21] The steamer *Bear River*, owned by the Bear River Steamship Company, carried much of the import-export trade to Saint John. The principal shareholders in the company were Clarke Brothers, giving them considerable control over the town's trade. They also owned schooners which brought back flour from Boston and molasses from the Caribbean. Local merchants acted as bankers, loaning money to farmers and taking goods such as butter, eggs, and lumber in repayment.[22] With their diverse interests, the town's merchants were keystones of the local economy.

Lumbering and Sawmilling

In the last third of the nineteenth century, the lumber trade developed alongside farming as a major staple of the Bear River economy. The extensive stands of softwoods that existed in the Bear River watershed had scarcely been touched up to the 1860s, largely because of their inaccessibility. But with the exhaustion of New England forests and growing demand for lumber from burgeoning industrial cities in the United States, it became economic to exploit them. During the peak years of production, in the 1890s and early 1900s, Bear River exported some 10,000,000 board feet annually, much of it to the United States.[23] "Planers" (air-dried, clear stock for woodworkers and builders), box-boards, staves for lime casks and apple barrels, barrel heads, sheathing, flooring, laths, cordwood, and piling were all shipped to Boston and New York. Hemlock bark was exported to Marblehead and Boston for the tanning industry, and pulpwood was sent to Havre de Grace, Maryland. In addition, there were important markets in South America and the Caribbean, particularly Cuba. Squared ship timber was also rafted up the Bay of Fundy to Hantsport for shipbuilding.[24] For return freights, Bear River vessels brought back flour from the United States and sugar and molasses from the Caribbean. Such links tied Bear River into an extensive Atlantic economy of trade and credit/debt relations.

Local interests controlled Bear River's lumber industry. Although farmers and small merchants participated in the trade, the Bear River firm of Clarke Brothers dominated much of the industry (Plates 14–15). Beginning in the dry goods business, the Clarkes invested in the timber trade and eventually became a successful, highly integrated firm. At the peak of their operations, they owned more than 10,000 acres of timberland, ran their own sawmill, and operated sailing vessels that carried lumber to market.[25] In Bear River, they owned all but two businesses along the Annapolis side of Main Street, giving rise to the name Clarke's Corner.[26] Among these premises were wharves, warehouses, and a general store, known as the "Trading Company," which supplied farmers and lumberers (Plate 16). In 1903, Clarke Brothers sold merchandise worth $131,000 and lumber, wood, and piling totaling $142,000.[27] Pillars of the local community, they were the "timber barons" of Bear River.

The assault on the softwood stands of Bear River was a seasonal, largely pre-industrial activity that employed many of the able-bodied men in the area. Clarkes employed more than 100 men in the woods, with a further 75 men at their mill.[28] Other men, working for piece-wages, hauled lumber from the mills to the wharves on the river. Many of the lumberers were farmers or farm laborers from Bear River. Work in the woods provided them with much-needed cash or store credit to help them survive on their marginal farms.[29] "Common laborers" received a dollar a day for a ten-hour day, the standard workday. "River drivers" were paid two dollars a day and "found" (room and board). With the outbreak of World War I wages rose, with some skilled workers making as much as $4 a day. In general, wages doubled, but "so did prices," recalled retired lumberman John Henshaw, "so we weren't any better off."[30]

Lumbering took place in the winter months, from about the middle of October to late March, with river-driving occurring in April.[31] As the pine stands were some ten miles from Bear River, Clarkes had five or six camps near Lake Joli and Lake Franklin, each housing about twenty men (Plates 17–18). Board was good in these logging camps, the menu consisting of plenty of beans, salt fish, potatoes, and beef, with dessert made up of "molasses on plain bread." The standard drink was "bootleg tea," so-called because of its black color, and it was taken without sugar or cream or milk.[32]

The methods and technology of lumbering in Bear River were still pre-industrial in the early years of the twentieth century, a reflection of the relatively low capital investment and small-scale operation involved. Unlike the industrial logging on the West Coast, which used donkey engines and railways, lumbering in Bear River relied on the muscle of men and animals. The lumber crews were divided into choppers, who cut down the trees, and teamsters, who hauled out the logs. A camp "boss" oversaw the crew. Trees were cut with single-bitted axes until 1908-10, when cross-cut saws were introduced (Plate 19). The use of cross-cut saws probably took place after Bear River men working in the woods of Maine and New Hampshire saw them used there.[33] After their limbs were stripped, the logs were loaded onto sleds (Plate 20), which were then hauled either by teams of horses or oxen direct to local mills, or yarded for the spring drive (Plates 21–22).[34] Oxen were used extensively in all woods operations. The working life of an ox team in these operations was not long. "Will" Miller, manager for Clarkes at Lake Joli, usually sold many of the older ox teams for beef each spring, and in the early fall went to "The French Shore" (Meteghan area) and bought enough younger teams to keep the logging going during the next winter. The fact that "you can beef them after they're too old to work" was one of the supposed advantages of oxen over horses.[35] After milling, teams laboriously hauled the lumber overland to shipping wharves in Bear River. A team with a typical load of 2,000 board feet took the best part of a day to cover the nine miles from the mills to the wharves.[36]

The application of industrial technology to lumbering had made most headway in sawmilling. Virtually all the timber cut in Bear River was milled before export, and many mills were steam powered. Although several portable mills with rotary saws powered by steam operated in the Bear River watershed, the largest mill, owned by the Clarkes, was permanently sited at Lake Joli, nine miles inland from Bear River on one of the "head" lakes of the West Branch (Plate 23). Three steam boilers powered rotary, stock, and gang saws, which operated from ice-out in the spring to freeze-up in the fall (Plate 24).[37] The mill handled 35,000 board feet a day, three to four million feet in a good season. After softwoods gave out in 1915, Clarkes cut hardwoods and added a dowel mill, a clothespin factory, and a sash-and-door factory (Plates 25–27). Such basic manufacturing added value to the product before export. Besides the mill, there was a cook house for the mill hands, storage sheds, and a dry-house. At the height of sawmilling operations before the First World War, some 200 people lived in Lake Joli and on the farms along the road to Morganville. The community had its own post office, and movies were shown at the mill on Saturday nights. Completely dependent on the mill, Lake Joli was a small company town in the forest.

Other mills in the Bear River area were much smaller, served local needs, and employed fewer men. Cunningham's mill, located on "The Flat" in Bear River (Plates 28–29), took its timber—"pasture spruce and popple [poplar]"—from local farmers and turned it into staves and heads for apple barrels, lime casks, fish drums, and nail kegs, as well as doing custom sawing. The mill sold much of its output in the Maritimes and never employed more than twenty men.[38] Several small mills, concentrated along Wade Brook, also produced carriages, caskets, and furniture, as well as doing carding and tanning (Plate 30).[39]

Shipbuilding and Shipping

The timber trade was a major stimulus to the local shipbuilding and shipping industry. Much of the wood for shipbuilding was available locally, and vessels were needed to carry lumber to market. During the 1870s and 1880s at least five shipyards operated in Bear River (Plate 31). They turned out barques, barkentines, brigantines, and schooners, although over time they built more schooners than square-riggers. This was largely an attempt to reduce costs. According to shipbuilder Reginald Benson, "the full-rigged ship needs a bigger crew—there's more gear to handle—and steam ships were giving sail competition so that freights were dropping. The schooner was cheaper to build and less expensive to man...three or four men could usually handle a small one, and the schooner had actually bigger hulls [sic] in proportion to rigging, so they could carry more pay load."[40] Besides shipbuilding, there was ship-repair work, particularly re-caulking, re-coppering, and painting (Plates 32–33).

Although shipbuilders imported bar iron, pitch, and tar, much of the lumber for shipbuilding came from the Bear River area. Knees or "angle timbers" for the vessel were sawn out of either black spruce or hackmatack (tamarack), although "hackmatack made the best knees." Knees were usually "cut out of the root and butt pieces." Most of the "frame of the vessel was made of oak, yellow birch, or spruce...but oak was best."[41] Reginald Benson recalled "there was lots of good oak for frame[s] down river, towards the bridges."[42] Because local timber was either too small or too brittle, shipbuilders in Bear River imported main masts and spars from the West Coast. In the 1860s and 1870s, the wood "came usually to Saint John and was Oregon pine either 'eight squared' or 'sixteen squared'...the spars were usually made complete in Saint John, then towed across the Bay of Fundy by the old *Citizen* [schooner] to Bear River," or "many times the finished hulls were towed from Bear River to Saint John and rigged there."[43] Later, Douglas fir imported from British Columbia was used for masts. According to Maurice Benson, "the Douglas fir was eight-squared on the

West Coast and shipped east in 80-foot sticks—it took three flat cars on a freight train to handle that length. The cars were unloaded at Bear River station and the sticks were hauled to town by ox-teams, or sometimes the big sticks were dumped overboard from the Victoria Bridges and towed up river to town."[44]

Considerable labor was needed to build a vessel. At its height, the shipbuilding industry in Bear River employed directly in the yards and indirectly in the fitting-out trades, more than one hundred men. The largest yard, John Benson's, employed twenty-five to thirty workers. Among this work force were hewers of timber, carpenters, caulkers, fitters, riggers, and common laborers or helpers. According to Reginald Benson, "everything for ships was manufactured in Bear River."[45] Blacksmiths—known as "ship smiths"—did the iron work, sail makers worked in the town's sail loft, and local women tailored oil skins for crews of Bear River vessels. Shipbuilding work was also laborious and used simple hand tools. While employed in the construction of the Clarke barkentine *Ethel Clarke,* ship carpenter Maurice Benson hewed the "main yard" from an 80-foot long spruce stick. The round stick was first squared, then "eight squared," and then "sixteen squared." "This work was all done with the broad-axe or adze...then we used the draw knife [to] rough round it," and finally "we planed it smooth round. It would take two men about three days from the rough log to the finished stick."[46] Wages in the shipyards were comparable to those in the woods. According to Al Marshall, "workers, such as caulkers and fitters got $1.50 a day, common labor $1.00 a day for a ten hour day...John Benson as a master builder got $3.00 a day."[47]

Much of the investment in the shipbuilding and shipping trades came from local merchants, shipbuilders, and prominent citizens of the town.[48] According to Al Marshall, the approximate cost of building one of the large barques was from $40,000 to $50,000, usually spread among several shareholders. Shipbuilder Reginald Benson, son of John Benson, recalled "there were 64 shares in a vessel, and my father usually got $1/16$ or $1/8$—sometimes buying the shares, sometimes getting them for bossing the job. Before a ship was built, people in town—like the Clarkes or Marshalls—would sign for shares—and sometimes folks from outside might sign up for a few. Then when the ship made a profit on her trip they'd split it according to the shares a man had. Sometimes a man might sign on the ship as captain on shares."[49] Multiple ownership lessened risks in a hazardous industry, particularly when owners rarely bought insurance. According to Marshall, "the rates were too high, and Father never had insurance—we'd rather lose a ship every seven years than have to pay the rates."[50] Clarke Brothers, too, did not always insure their vessels; in 1900, their schooner *Muriel* went down without any coverage.[51]

All the lumber exported from Bear River was shipped by water. In the heyday of the industry, the wharves in Bear River were loaded with wood (Plates 34–38), and "the river was full of ships waiting to take on cargoes."[52] "I've seen more than 3 million feet of lumber on Bear River wharves at one time," recalled Roy Miller, "but that was when the lumber mills were going full speed." The Clarke-owned schooners *Neva* and *Valdare,* which "were always going back and forth to Boston," carried much of the lumber (Plate 39). "Once in awhile we'd get a big ship in, a barque maybe—that would take as much as a million feet in one load. She'd load up at the wharf with all they'd dare put on, then she'd top out a deck load at Peck's Hole [just above the Victoria Bridge] with lumber that had been towed down with her on a barge."[53] Virtually the last lumber shipped from Bear River was in 1917-1918, "some of it for Halifax," to help with rebuilding the city after the explosion.[54]

Working Away

The traditional economy of farming, lumbering, shipbuilding, and shipping could not employ all the available labor in Bear River. From at least the late nineteenth century, young men and women had been leaving Bear River in search of seasonal jobs.[55] Some men found work locally. Log drives on the Tusket River in southwest Nova Scotia employed Bear River "white water" men for two months in the spring.[56] "Wilkie Rice took charge on the Tusket," remembered lumberman John Henshaw, who "went with him eleven springs." The drive usually lasted 60 or 70 days, and as "we got $2 a day and 'found' we had money in our pockets when we got home."[57] Across the Bay of Fundy, Bear River men cut wood at Musquash, New Brunswick.[58] Farther away, men worked on ice-teams in Boston during the summer months,[59] and others took CPR "harvest specials" to the Prairies to bring in the wheat.[60] Women worked as domestics in Boston and Cambridge, or in the shoe shops of Lynn.[61]

The frequent moves of Enoch Peck well illustrate the peripatetic life led by many young people from Bear River. At an early age, sometime before the First World War, Peck left Bear River to work on the farm of a cousin near Waterville, Maine, where he stayed for two or three years. From there, he took a job as a "shop repair man" for the street car company that operated an electric line in Central Maine between Waterville, Augusta, and Lewiston. Later, he worked for a time in the Hollingsworth and Whitney Paper mill in Waterville, and then went to Nakomis, Saskatchewan, where a sister and her husband were "homesteading" a 160-acre wheat farm. At the outbreak of the First World War, Peck returned home to enlist in the Canadian army, together with a younger brother, and went overseas in February 1915. Following his demobilization, he went to Forest City, New Brunswick, where he met his wife, and settled there for several years. Eventually, he returned to Bear River and settled on the family farm.[62]

Those living in the "Boston States" kept in touch with friends and family. Alice Peck, Ed McKay's mother, moved from Bear River to Boston in 1881 and there worked as a pastry cook in Thompson's Spa restaurant on Washington Street. Sometime after her husband's unexpected early death, she sent her young son back to Bear River to stay with her parents to get a grade-school education. With her sister, also working in Boston, she sent a portion of her earnings back to her parents to help with household expenses. Although her son lived for awhile in Bear River, she could only afford to visit "home" every two or three years. When she retired, she moved to Winslow, Maine, to spend her last days on a farm which was owned by a younger brother, Orin.[63]

Al Marshall, who worked for Jordan Marsh Company in Boston for eleven years before returning to Bear River to take over the family business, "used to go to the Common every Sunday after church to what we called the Nova Scotia Corner [near the site of the present bandstand] and meet with the Bensons, Hinxmans and others from Bear River...sometimes there would be 150 or more of us at the Nova Scotia Corner just talking and visiting.... A group of us always went down to the Yarmouth boat in the early morning to see who might be coming from home." Many of these Bear River people lived in Cambridge or Somerville.[64] "If you took the Nova Scotians out of Somerville," observed Reginald Benson, himself a migrant from Bear River to Boston and a resident of Somerville, "there wouldn't be much city left."[65]

A Local World

For many inhabitants, Bear River was a familiar place, a community of known people. Immigration into the area had finished in the 1830s, and some four generations of settlers had grown up. A handful of surnames—Harris, Parker, Rice, Clarke, Benson, Peck—accounted for much of the population. Kinship ties were close, binding people into the community and to past generations. Face-to-face interaction characterized many economic and social activities. Work forces were small, and only a few merchants handled the town's business. Employers and employees, merchants and farmers got to know each other. Mutual aid and help were common on farms, particularly at harvest time. Most of the population belonged to church congregations—predominantly Baptist, Methodist, and Adventist—and these put on social events, such as teas, bake-sales, and harvest suppers. Friendly societies, such as the Masons and Oddfellows, attracted tradesmen, farmers, and merchants (Plate 40). Farmers supported the annual agricultural exhibition, held in the Digby County Exhibition Hall on the west side of the village. And once a year, the entire community came together to celebrate the Cherry Carnival, a festival of bands, parades, and sports (Plates 41–42).

The leaders of the community lived in Bear River and were well known. Between 1900 and the mid-1930s, the Clarkes, the Marshalls, and the town physician and federal liberal member of parliament, L.J. Lovett, made up the elite group in Bear River. All three families were related by marriage and dominated much of the town's economic, political, and social life. Willard G. Clarke served as councillor on the Annapolis Municipal Council (an important position as Bear River was unincorporated), participated in the Nova Scotia liberal party, and joined his brothers Wallace and Bernard on the Bear River Board of Trade. As an unincorporated town, the Board of Trade served as a *de facto* town council, responsible for promoting business and looking after social welfare. Wallace Clarke also served on the town's school board. Both Willard and Wallace were Masons and gave land to the lodge to allow it to expand.[66] With merchant A.B. Marshall and Dr. Lovett, Willard Clarke also supported the Bear River Brass Band, one of the main entertainment features in the town's annual festival, the Cherry Carnival.[67] "We used to put on Cherry Carnivals for years" remembered Marshall, "and we never thought so much about what we were going to get out of it, but about doing our best to have a good time for the day."[68]

Many of these economic and social activities took place at "The Bridge." Edgar McKay remembers "as far back as 1918, but more likely the mid-1930s when [he] was frequently 'home for the summer'—the stores were generally crowded with men, women, and children. Groups stood outside the stores in little knots, chatting, gossiping, visiting with friends and relatives they had not seen for a week or perhaps two. People in those days would not be from Bear River only, but from Lake Joli, Morganville, Greenland, Victory, Bear River East, Clementsvale, Lansdowne, and the Sissiboo Road—all the surrounding areas—the roads like the spokes of a wheel converging on the hub—'the Bridge'—on Saturday night. Many of those who came with ox or horse drawn wagons had left home early so as to have time to shop and visit as well" (Plate 43).[69]

People in Bear River lived and worked within a localized time. Although clocks, standard time, and ten-hour days were all used in Bear River, natural processes influenced rhythms of life and work. Seasonal and daily fluctuations of weather and tide were vitally important to an economy based on farming, lumbering, and sailing ships (Plates 44–45). Even in the Lake Joli sawmill—the largest industrial operation in the area—the work was seasonal and men left the mill in July to bring in the hay.[70] Travel, too, depended on the seasonal state of roads and river (Plates 46–47). According to the Bear River newspaper, the *Telephone,* 66 percent of travel was conducted in the six months between May and October; travel almost came to a stop in the winter month of February and mud season of March (Figure 4).[71] Roads were not regularly plowed in winter. "No cars can be used" reported the *Digby Courier* in December 1933, "and the horses have to do

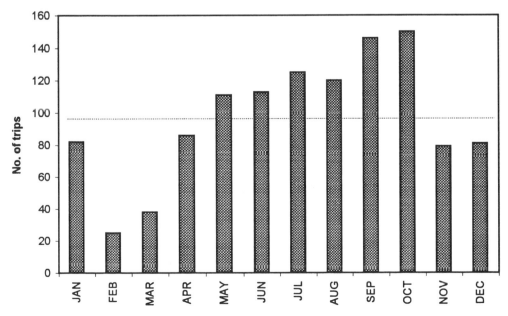

Fig. 4. Total monthly trips taken from Bear River, 1900-1902. (Bear River Telephone)

all the work."[72] Seasons demarcated the annual round of activities, while weather and tide influenced daily routine. "Work, woven with weather," remembered novelist Ernest Buckler, "was the very grain of existence."[73]

Local knowledge, too, was important. Many inhabitants of Bear River had intimate knowledge not only of their surrounding fields and woods but also the country inland from Bear River. In the back country, they cut hay from wild meadows, caught trout in countless lakes and streams, picked blueberries from burnt-over areas, and hunted moose and deer in the woods. Fields, meadows, woods, lakes, and streams were known and named. Names such as "Parker Meadow," "Peck Hill," and "Annie Morehouse Lake" inscribed family histories onto the landscape, connecting people to land, past to present. Such knowledge, useless beyond Bear River, helped bind people to place.[74]

Yet Bear River was not impervious to the outside world. The wood, wind, and sail economy of the town was situated in the much larger commercial arena of the North Atlantic. Prices of farm produce, lumber, flour, and store goods followed market rates set in Saint John and American east coast ports. Ties of credit and debt bound local farmers and lumberers to Bear River merchants who, in turn, were dependent on outside suppliers. Downswings in the market for produce or lumber led to squeezes on the chain of credit; debts were eventually called in. Clarke Brothers amassed part of their land holdings through unpaid debts and failed mortgages.

There was also some outside institutional involvement in the town. The federal government provided a post office and customs house, as well as subsidies to the Bear River Steamship Company.[75] In the immediate area, it also improved Digby Harbour and supported the building of the Dominion Atlantic Railway. Although much of Bear River's trade went to the United States and the Caribbean, this federal involvement in communications and transportation were early attempts to tie Bear River into the larger Canadian national economy. The federal government was also responsible for the Micmac reservation and provided Indian families with a small monthly allowance for the purchase of "store goods" in Bear River. The provincial government entered the local community through its control of education, responsibility for criminal and civil law, and provision of road monies. Besides the roads, this involvement was largely passive, a regulatory framework that lay in the background of everyday life.

Something of the cultural world of the northeastern United States and British Empire filtered into Bear River. The architecture of the town reflected historic ties to New England. The early settlers brought methods of building construction and styles of architecture from New England, and the economic and cultural dominance of Boston over western Nova Scotia during the nineteenth century reinforced this heritage.[76] Most buildings in Bear River had wood frame construction, clapboard siding, and shingled roofing. The prevailing architectural style in town was classical revival, particularly evident on the stores along Main Street. Most of these buildings turned their gable ends towards the street, a faint echo of the Greek temple front.[77] The spires of the Methodist and Baptist churches also took their cue from classical revival Episcopal and Congregational churches in New

England. A few buildings sported mansard roofs, a French Second Empire style that probably found its way into Bear River through American pattern books.

The local newspaper, the Bear River *Telephone,* reported on American news, as well as British imperial adventures overseas, particularly the Boer War. When Queen Victoria died in January 1901, the *Telephone* covered the story in great detail; the town's churches, draped in black crepe and Union Jacks, held memorial services; church, school, and town bells tolled for an hour; and flags on the stores of Clarke Brothers and A.B. Marshall, as well as some private residences, flew at half mast.[78] Patriotic sentiment for Empire ran strong. The *Telephone* also carried popular fiction, again usually by British or American authors. Canadian news rarely went beyond reporting about the federal government. At least from the perspective of the local newspaper, the newsworthy world extended either east across the Atlantic to Great Britain or southwest to the United States. Central and Western Canada were, for the most part, *terra incognita.*

The inhabitants of Bear River also traveled beyond the town. The "Local and Personal" columns of the *Telephone* provide considerable insight into this movement. Although business and professional classes may be over-represented, the columns give an indication of the size, geographic range, and time of travel. Between 1900 and 1902, the *Telephone* recorded 1,156 journeys away from Bear River. The average number of trips per year was 191 for men and 194 for women. Compared to the total population of Bear River, relatively few people were traveling. In 1901, the population of Bear River and Hillsburgh was 1,824. That year, the *Telephone* recorded 389 trips made by 217 individuals. Even allowing for under counting by the newspaper, remarkably few people in Bear River had traveled beyond the area that year.

The impressionistic evidence of seasonal employment suggests that people traveled in southwest Nova Scotia, across the Bay of Fundy to Saint John, and down the Gulf of Maine to Boston, with occasional forays to Manitoba. The *Telephone* largely confirms these patterns. According to the "Local and Personal" columns, most travel was to towns in southwest Nova Scotia, Saint John, or Boston. As Figure 5 shows, 55 percent of trips were made within southwest Nova Scotia, most of them to places in Annapolis Valley (Annapolis, Bridgetown, Round Hill, Granville, Middleton, Wolfville), around Annapolis Basin (Clementsport, Smiths Cove, Digby), or along the southwest coast (Weymouth, Meteghan, Yarmouth). Ninety-three trips were made to Saint John, the regional metropolis, compared to only thirty-four to Halifax, the provincial capital. Connections by boat across the Bay of Fundy were much more important than those by road and rail to Halifax. Beyond Nova Scotia and the Bay of Fundy, 28 percent of journeys were to the United States, more than half of them to Boston. A few trips were made to other parts of the Maritimes (Amherst, Sackville, Charlottetown), but scarcely any to Central and Western Canada (Montreal, Manitoba). Overall, the geographic world of those inhabitants who traveled beyond Bear River was limited to towns between Yarmouth and Wolfville (a distance of no more than seventy-five miles either side of

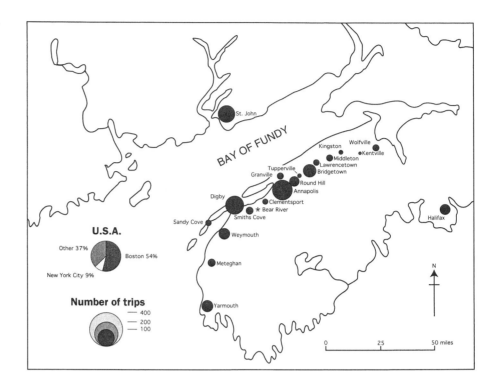

Fig. 5. Travel destinations of Bear River residents, 1900-1902 (Bear River Telephone)

Bear River) and the Bay of Fundy-Gulf of Maine axis. People looked outward to a maritime world of ships and ports rather than a continental world of trains and stations. For most inhabitants of Bear River, Saint John and Boston were clearly in view, but Halifax and Central Canada were beyond the horizon.[79]

Although the newspaper rarely listed reasons for travel, much local travel was either for business or visiting, while more distant travel, especially to the United States, was to find seasonal or permanent employment. Certainly, trips by tradesmen, merchants, and professionals made up between a quarter and a third of all male travel.[80] Most likely much of the long-distance travel for seasonal employment was undertaken by people in their late teens and early twenties. A study of out-migration from Canning at the eastern end of Annapolis Valley between 1868 and 1893 revealed that the most common age of migrants was between 18 and 22 years.[81] Because of the similarities in economy and society between Bear River and Canning, it is unlikely that Bear River migrants were much different.

Of the travelers from Bear River to the United States, 60 percent of women and 47 percent of men went to Boston. In the Canning study, the proportion was 59 percent and 46 percent, a remarkable similarity.[82] This difference between the genders was largely because women traveled only short distances to find work, allowing them to maintain ties with the parental home, whereas men traveled farther afield and set up new households.[83]

The newspaper evidence from Bear River clarifies the paradoxical impression of considerable geographical mobility and persistent localism found among the population of Bear River (and, indeed, much of Nova Scotia) during the age of wood, wind, and sail.[84] The evidence suggests that

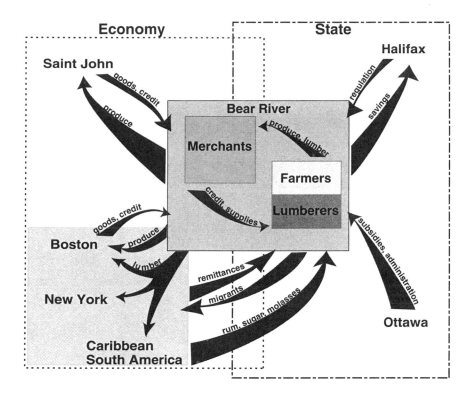

the bulk of the population of Bear River traveled relatively little and over short distances. These people were mostly farmers and artisans tied by work to the Bear River area. The remainder, including businessmen, professionals, and young people, traveled more frequently and over longer distances. For the young migrants leaving Bear River to find work, long-distance travel was part of the life-cycle. A short period of mobility to look for work was followed by a more sedentary life when a job had been found. Thus both the high degree of mobility that existed for a section of the population and the enduring localism of much of the rest become understandable, and the paradox is resolved.

Through the nineteenth century and first years of the twentieth century, Bear River sat on the physical, economic, social, and political edge of Nova Scotia and the rest of Canada (Figure 6). American and English immigrants had settled the valley largely because it offered ready access to the North Atlantic. The products of their farms, forests, shipyards, and workshops funneled into a maritime economy that stretched from the Bay of Fundy through the Gulf of Maine to the Caribbean and beyond. Controlling much of this trade were the town's merchants, standing with one foot in the local world of Bear River and another in the maritime world of the North Atlantic. They were the power-brokers, dominating the economic, social, and political life of the town. Migrants from Bear River looking for work followed trade routes to Boston, establishing a web of personal and family ties across the Gulf of Maine. Although Halifax and Ottawa had various political responsibilities over the community, their power was relatively weak. Economic and social ties also were limited. Bear River was an export enclave, looking outward to the sea with its back turned to the continental interior.

Bear River Country, 1890–1920

1. Bear River village looking southeast, c.1910-1912. This view shows Oakdene Academy and Methodist Church (now the United Church) at the end of Main Street; the town cemetery on the hillside; and Clarke Brothers store, warehouses, and wharves occupying the center of the business district. All these buildings are on the Annapolis side of the river. Ralph Harris's store and studio are to right of the large building with mansard roof on the Digby or Hillsburgh side of the river. The area where the bandstand and small boathouse are located was the Quigley shipyard, one of the earliest shipyards in the village.

2. Bear River village looking west, c.1908-1909. This view shows lumber wharves on the Digby side of the river, several stores built out over the river on pilings, and the Baptist Church on the hillside. To the left of the church is a barn-like building that served as a sail loft in the 1880s, the Hillsburgh School House in the 1890s, and as a drill hall for the local platoon of the 219th Battalion, Nova Scotia Highland Brigade, in 1915-1916.

3. Main Street in Bear River village looking west, c.1919-1920. Several stores have their gable ends facing the street, reflecting the influence of American classical revival architecture. Clarke Brothers store is on the left.

4. Bear River village looking south, c.1915. This view shows the swing bridge over the river, the steamer *Bear River* tied up alongside Clarke Brothers wharf, the Baptist Church, cleared fields and farms, and forested back country. Because of the steepness of the river bank, many buildings were built on sloping sites and had to be either cut into the hillside or built up on the down slope side.

5. Bear River 1905. This early view shows the considerable clearance that had taken place on the granite hills to the south of the village during the nineteenth century. Today, much of this area is forested. (Vernon Harris family album)

6. Byron Harris farm, near Bear River, c.1910-1912. This scene shows the typical method of "making hay," using a combination of horse-drawn hay rake and hand labor, on one of the larger farms at the turn of the century. Many smaller farms were not mechanized, and all hay making was done by hand.

7. Byron Harris farm, near Bear
River, c.1905. Byron Harris
putting mangle beets on a cart,
assisted by Lovett Apt. Byron
Harris generally raised 500
bushels of mangles and 1,000
bushels of turnips a year, mostly
for cattle feed, although some
turnips were shipped via
Yarmouth to the Boston market.
Byron Harris was the father of
photographer, Ralph Harris.

8. Cherry picking on the Bernard C. Clarke property in Bear River village c.1910. Bernard Clarke was a brother of W.G. and W.W. Clarke and worked for them as store clerk.

9. The W.G. Clarke apple orchard, near Bear River, c.1905-1910. Fowler Robinson, caretaker of the orchard, is shown spraying apples. The Clarke orchard was the largest in Bear River and frequently produced 500 bbls. of apples a year.

10. The Joseph L. Warren farm, Annapolis side of Bear River, c.1910-1912. Joe Warren is shown picking strawberries, which he sold in Bear River, Smiths Cove, and Digby. He also had a sizeable apple orchard and raised some potatoes for market.

11. The Thaddeus Harris farm c.1910. Thad Harris is collecting sap from his "maple orchard." Note the wooden hollowed troughs for gathering sap and the wooden home-made "spiles" in trees. Harris sold syrup and sugar locally.

12. Looking east along the main street
    in the village of Bear River, early
    twentieth century. The close rela-
    tionship between land and sea is
    clearly shown by the vessels moored
    in the heart of the town.

13. The steamer *Bear River* between the
    bridges at the mouth of Bear River,
    November 1919. From 1905 until
    withdrawal from service in the
    1930s, she was the principal means
    of transport between Bear River and
    Saint John. Apart from weekly
    crossings of the Bay of Fundy, she
    did towage work up and down Bear
    River and around Annapolis Basin.
    In this photograph she is shown
    loaded with barrels of apples bound
    for Saint John.

14. Four generations of the Clarke family posed before the neo-classical grandeur of the W.G. Clarke residence, Bear River, c.1919. Standing, from left to right: Mr. W.G. Clarke, holding grandson William MacIntyre; Mrs. W.G. Clarke. Seated in wicker chair: Mrs. Richard Clarke, mother of W.G. Clarke. Seated on steps: Mrs. Gordon A. MacIntyre, née Josephine Clarke; Gordon A. MacIntyre, a principal promoter of the Bear River pulp mill in 1919-1920. Although this photograph shows Bear River's leading family at the height of its prosperity, the bankruptcy of Clarke Brothers four years later gives it considerable poignancy. The little Clarke grandson would not inherit his grandfather's fortune and position in Bear River society.

15. The W.W. Clarke residence, Bear River village, c.1920. W.W. Clarke was a member of the firm Clarke Brothers, and his wife was the daughter of Harden Chute, a wealthy Bear River merchant. In immaculate condition, the house stood a few steps from Clarke Brothers store. Note the hunting trophy on the porch wall

16. Bear River Trading Company c.1919-1920. This store was known as Clarke Brothers Ltd for many years, but the name was changed at the time the Bear River Pulp Company was organized. It was the major store in the village in the early twentieth century, a conduit through which goods came into and out of Bear River. (Edgar McKay Collection # 1992-450.86 Public Archives of Nova Scotia)

17. Logging camp, Lake Joli, February 1920. This shows one of the half-dozen logging camps maintained by Clarke Brothers in the Lake Joli region. The composition and size of the group (numbers of men, horses, and oxen) is quite typical of these camps. Such male work camps set in the wilderness and dependent on an export staple trade were important components of the early pattern of Canadian settlement.

18. Teamsters with their horse teams, Lake Franklin camp, c.1911. Logging camps usually had three or four teams of horses and three or four yoke of oxen to carry supplies into the camps and haul logs out of the woods to the landings for the spring drive to the mill. The teamsters are from left to right: Gus Dunn, Fred Porter, Boyd Rice, and Jack Milner.

19. This shows the typical method and technology of logging in the Lake Joli region, c.1920. Logging relied on the muscle of men for chopping and sawing, ox teams for hauling, and a simple technology of axes and cross-cut saws. Apart from the recent introduction of cross-cut saws, logging practices had not changed in the area since the eighteenth century.

20. One of the Clarke Brothers logging yards in the Lake Joli area, c.1920. Photograph shows men loading hardwood logs on horse sleds for hauling to the mill. As hardwood logs do not float, they had to be taken overland to the mills.

21. Ox teams, Lake Franklin Camp, c.1911. From foreground to background, the teamsters are Arthur Brown, Ellsworth McSwain, Clarence Morgan (right of McSwain), Boyd Rice, David McLean, and Fletcher Milbury.

22. Lake Joli region, c.1920. Hauling hardwood logs to the Clarke Brothers hardwood mill at Lake Joli. Gilbert Hubley, woods boss for the Clarkes, is shown far right. Note the superb condition of the horses, an absolute necessity for efficient operations.

23. Lake Joli softwood mill, c.1908. The large building, with the porch, on the roadside, was the cook house, where many mill workers boarded and had bunks on the top floor. The mill is to the right. Owned by Clarkes, Lake Joli was a small company town in the wilderness.

24. Lake Joli hardwood mill, 25 June 1920. Log carriage in the hardwood mill, manned from left to right by Ross McCormick, unknown person, and Frank Gehu, the "tail-stocker" who rolled logs onto the carriage.

25. Lake Joli hardwood mill, 1920. Buildings from left to right include the clothespin factory, the dowel mill, and the barn.

26. Lake Joli hardwood mill, February 1920. The block-like building directly to the right of the stack was the sash-and-door factory, the dowel mill was to the right and front, and the clothespin factory occupied the highest part of the structure on the right.

27. Lake Joli hardwood mill, February 1920. Frank Gehu and Alfred Cashman making dowels.

28. Cunningham's mill at "The Flat" or "Head of the Tide" in Bear River village, 1920. This photograph shows on the left Cunningham's sawmill drawing logs from the mill pond, in the middle a grist mill and machinery for making staves, on the right a shed used for storage, packing, and processing, and on the extreme right an office and store. Like other mills in the Bear River area, Cunningham's mill used steam to power the saws, which allowed it to operate all year.

29. Cunningham's mill at "The Flat" in Bear River village, c.1927. The picture shows the mill on the right, with staves stacked under sheds and outside, as well as sawed lumber.

30. "The Flat" in Bear River village, c.1920, showing the concentration of mills at the junction of the East (on extreme left) and West Branches of the Bear River. On the left is Thelbert Rice's monument works, which had machinery powered by water wheel. A wagon loaded with apple barrels, probably made at nearby Cunningham's mill, stands in front of the works. On the right, behind the smoke-stack, is a grist mill that ground grain as late as 1920, while on the extreme right is part of Cunningham's sawmill.

31. Bear River village, c.1890. This early view shows the John Benson ship-yard on the left and the Tom Rice shipyard near the Bridge, as well as the road to Lansdowne, the Digby side of the village, and the Digby County Exhibition Hall on the extreme right. Shipbuilding required little infrastructure. A ship builder needed access to tidewater, a saw pit, a steam-box, some simple hand tools, and little else. (Public Archives of Nova Scotia)

32. A barkentine being towed stern first by motor launch after repairs at the Tom Rice yard in the foreground, c.1912.

33. The Reginald Benson shipyard, Clarke's Marsh, Bear River, 1920/21. One of the last ship repair jobs done in Bear River was repairing a steam tug owned by the Dominion Coal Company. Reg Benson estimated that "about a dozen men were employed on the repair job for two months." Reg Benson was the son of shipbuilder John Benson, whose brother Zebulon "Zeb" Benson is shown on the stern of the tug. Zeb's son, Maurice, is also in the picture but cannot be identified.

34. The landscape of wood, wind, and sail. This classic photograph encapsulates much of the settlement and economy of early twentieth-century Bear River as well as a good deal of Maritime Canada. The schooners loading lumber at the Government Wharf (foreground) and Clarke wharf (middle ground) illustrate the staple economies of lumber and shipping, while the wooden, framed stores, churches, school (right), and hillside farms with their apple orchards (background) show a typical Maritime agricultural community. Only the steamer *Bear River* introduces an industrial element to the scene.

35. The heyday of shipping lumber, c.1905. The river is full of vessels, either loading lumber or carrying cargoes down river on the flood tide. The schooner *Citizen*, which made weekly runs to Saint John before the introduction of the steamer, is probably the vessel in the foreground.

36. Vessels loading lumber at the Government Wharf (foreground) and Clarke Brothers wharf (background).

37. A close-up of the three vessels loading lumber at Clarke Brothers wharf shown in Plate 36.

38. Looking towards the Digby side of Bear River, early twentieth century. A barkentine is loading lumber at the Government Wharf.

39. A schooner, high in the water, coasting down river, early twentieth century.

40. The town band leads members of Keith Masonic Lodge in a parade, Bear River village, c.1913. The Grand Central House is on the left, flying British and Canadian flags. (Public Archives of Nova Scotia)

41. Cherry carnival parade, Bear River village, 1925.

42. Water sports at the Cherry Carnival, Bear River village, c.1920. Traditional water sports included swimming, canoe racing, walking the greased pole, log rolling, canoe tilting, and tub racing.

43. Murray Harris and his "dagon" ox, Main Street, Bear River village, c.1905. A "dagon" ox is one trained to work singly with yoke or harness, although harness as shown in this photograph was rare with oxen. Harris brought vegetables to town in this conveyance. Marshall's store is in the center background.

44. Lumber vessel at high tide, Bear River village, early twentieth century. Normal rise of tide at this point is about 13 feet, with especially high tides rising to nearly 15 feet in the spring and fall. (Stirling County Study Series B, 4.2 Public Archives of Nova Scotia)

45. Lumber vessel at low tide, Bear River village, early twentieth century. (Stirling County Study Series B, 4.2 Public Archives of Nova Scotia)

46. A typical winter scene on Main Street in Bear River village (Digby side) c.1910-1912. Oxen and horses were used exclusively up to this time for cartage of goods by land. The first automobile was not owned in town until the autumn of 1913 and without snow ploughing would have been useless from December to March.

47. Steamer *Bear River* stuck in ice, 14 February 1914. The steamer remained stuck for two weeks before hot water from the boiler was used to melt sufficient ice to let the vessel settle down. John Morine, fireman, is second from right.

2

Contours of Change 1890–1950

F ROM the perspective of the early 1950s, the "golden age" of Bear River was before the First World War, when it was "a busy town." After that, Bear River went into decline. By the 1930s, it was a place where people were "waiting for something to turn up."[1] By then, Bear River was hemorrhaging population, and its traditional sectors of farming, lumbering, shipbuilding, and shipping were in steep decline. Meanwhile, the increasing press of outside forces—corporate capital, the state, tourism, modern communications—were reshaping the town. The combination of these processes transformed Bear River.

The contours of these demographic and economic changes can be sketched briefly. As Figure 7 shows, the population of Bear River reached its peak in 1881 and then began to fall, especially after 1891. It recovered slightly only in the early 1940s.[2] The decrease was most marked in Hillsburgh, the predominantly rural part of Bear River, where marginal farms in the back country were abandoned. The village of Bear River and the more fertile agricultural area to the northeast saw only modest decline. The economic collapse can be charted using Dun & Bradstreet credit books.[3] Although Figure 8 reveals an almost uninterrupted decrease in the number of businesses between 1900 and 1950, it also shows that capitalization of Bear River businesses reached a peak in 1920 and then fell dramatically. Essentially, these figures document the rise and fall of Clarke Brothers, and with them the economy of much of the town. Together, the demographic and economic evidence suggest that Bear River saw an absolute decrease in population from the 1880s but this was ameliorated to some extent by economic expansion in the lumber industry. When this industry collapsed in the 1920s, there was little left in Bear River to arrest the decline; only outside intervention by the state and a growing tourist trade helped check the slide.

The decline in the population of Bear River reflected the collapse of the traditional economy and lure of better-paying jobs elsewhere.[4] In the agricultural sector, the number of farms in Bear River and Hillsburgh fell from 337 to 133 between 1891 and 1941, with Hillsburgh losing two-thirds of its farms (from 206 to 68). The total area of occupied land shrank from 36,218 to 15,099 acres, and the area of improved land contracted from

Opposite: A dramatic view from the tracks of the Dominion Atlantic Railway of Clarke Bothers kraft pulp mill under construction, c.1919-1920.

10,467 to 7,556 acres. Numbers of cattle and sheep also declined. Although farms of all sizes decreased, the greatest decline was in farms of fewer than 11 acres. Comprising 42 percent of all farms in 1891, they made up only 6 percent fifty years later.[5]

Local and regional factors lay behind this contraction. The collapse of the lumber industry in Bear River during the 1920s left many small farmers, who had worked in the woods and mills, without any income. As a result, many farms, particularly those located in the Hillsburgh back country, were

Fig. 7. *Population of Bear River, 1871-1941. (Census of Canada)*

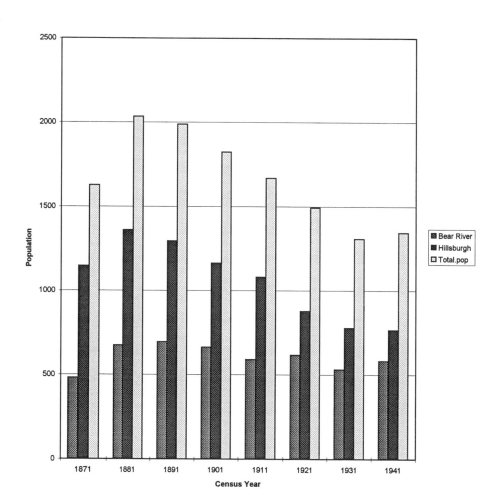

Fig. 8. *Estimated maximum capitalization of businesses in Bear River, 1900-1950. (Dun & Bradstreet Reference Book)*

$	500,000 - 750,000	300,000 - 500,000	50,000 - 75,000	35,000 - 50,000	10,000 - 20,000	5,000 - 10,000	3,000 - 5,000	2,000 - 3,000	1,000 - 2,000	500 - 1,000	Less than 500	Total Businesses	Total Max. Capitalization
1900					1*	3	5	4	6	4	14	37	110,000
1910			1*			5	8	2	6	2	4	28	162,000
1920	1*	1	1*		2	4(1*)	5	4	2	3	9	32	1,453,500
1930					2		5	2	7	1	3	29	87,500
1940					1	2	2	2	3	1	5	16	65,500
1950						3	2	1	3	4	3	16	96,500

*Clarke Brothers Business

abandoned.[6] By 1954, there were twenty-one places "tore down" between Lake Joli and Morganville.[7] More generally, agriculture in the Maritimes, pressured by producers in other regions, was becoming increasingly specialized. Farms on good land close to markets prospered, supplying milk, butter, eggs, soft fruits, and vegetables to Halifax, Saint John, and other urban centers; those on marginal land far from market found it difficult to compete.[8] In Bear River, many farms were too small and hilly to be mechanized, while lack of feed and hay limited dairying.[9] A creamery, set up in 1904, soon failed.[10] Moreover, declining overseas markets for apples, and the ravages of the browntail moth in the 1920s curtailed fruit growing (Plate 1). Some farmers continued to supply a range of dairy goods, vegetables, and fruit to urban markets, while others either gave up farming or diversified as best they could. In the 1920s, at least one farmer turned to silver fox ranching, "almost a dozen" began chicken farming, and a few, near Deep Brook, raised seed turnips.[11] By 1945, farmers were also harvesting Christmas trees.[12] Except for seed turnips, these products did not require good land and all were destined for specialized urban markets.

After the heyday of shipbuilding in the 1870s and 1880s, the industry, like that in the rest of the Maritimes, contracted rapidly. Introduction of steam vessels, falling freight rates, and alternative investment opportunities in manufacturing and railways all undermined the industry. The last vessel built in Bear River was lost on its maiden voyage in 1901.[13] After that, shipyards closed or worked sporadically on ship repairs. By 1925, there was no shipyard left in town.[14]

Shipping, too, declined. By 1906, merchants A.B. Marshall and W.A. Chute had sold off their vessels, leaving only Clarke Brothers as shipowners in Bear River.[15] After Clarkes sold their large barkentine in 1912, they owned only two schooners for coasting and the steamer *Bear River* for the Saint John run.[16] Because of the large amount of surplus shipping in the Maritimes, Clarkes increasingly chartered vessels to carry lumber to market. The bankruptcy of Clarkes in the early 1920s ended the shipping industry in Bear River. With only a few vessels calling to load pulp logs, the customs office closed in 1935.[17]

The lumber and sawmilling industries were also squeezed. Lumbermen had cut over softwoods by 1914, and exhausted hardwoods by the early 1920s. The Lake Joli hardwood mill burnt down in 1923—some said it was an insurance fire—and was not rebuilt. Bear River's last remaining sawmill—a box and stave mill—along with a "large block of timberland" was sold in 1943 to International Cooperage of Niagara, Ontario, a subsidiary of an American company.[18] The mill closed eleven years later, a victim of technological change in the packing industry.

To avert collapse of the Bear River economy, the town's mercantile elite turned to railways and manufacturing as new cornerstones of the economy.[19] By providing links to landward markets, a railway would reorient Bear River towards the rest of Nova Scotia and connect it to Central and Western Canada. Between 1904 and 1916, local businessmen threw their support behind two railway schemes. One wanted to link Liverpool on the South Shore with the Dominion Atlantic Railway in the Annapolis Valley, while the other planned to connect Shelburne with Digby. Both railways would have had to cross the rocky, lake-strewn, and largely uninhabited backbone of Nova Scotia before dropping into the Bear River Valley to make connection with the Dominion Atlantic. As railroad magnates Mackenzie and Mann were involved in the Halifax & South Western Railway, local promoters hoped the Central Canadians would support the new ventures. MacKenzie and Mann were not tempted, however, and nothing came of either proposal.[20] Bear River remained four miles from the nearest railway, unconnected to the railway system of the continent.

Bear River merchants also looked to the expanding pulp and paper industry to replace the failing timber trade.[21] Much more than the old clothespin and sash-and-door factories at Lake Joli, a pulp mill would take Bear River into the industrial age and tie the town into the rapidly expanding pulpwood trade of western Nova Scotia. In 1904, Clarke Brothers bid unsuccessfully for the Sissiboo Pulp & Paper Company in neighboring Weymouth.[22] In 1912, Clarkes became a public limited company, capitalized at $300,000, which placed them in a better position to raise capital for industrial development.[23] Although Clarkes discussed building a sulphite mill in Bear River in 1913,[24] the First World War disrupted plans. Clarkes renewed interest only in 1919.[25] To ease the change from mercantile family to industrial corporation, Clarke Brothers formed limited companies for their lumber business (Clarke Brothers Limited of Canada), retail store (Bear River Trading Company Limited), fruit packing (Bear River Fruit Company Limited), and new pulp mill (Bear River Pulp Company Limited).[26] Building the mill, estimated to cost $1,500,000, required substantial outside financing.[27] Clarkes took out a mortgage with the Nova Scotia Trust Company and sold bonds on the Toronto and New York markets. Perkins, Goodwin & Co., a paper making firm based in New York City, bought some of these bonds.[28] The composition of the board of directors of the mill reflected this mix of local and continental capital. Alongside members of the Clarke family sat Charles T. Starke, a partner in the Toronto-based investment house of John Starke & Co., which dealt in corporation securities and real estate.[29] For the first time in their business history, Clarkes were reliant on a considerable infusion of external capital.

Using second-hand brick from a demolished mill in Saint John and machinery from a mill in the American South, Clarkes built the pulp mill on tide water at the entrance to Bear River (Plates 2–3). The mill was designed to manufacture kraft pulp for shipment across the Bay of Fundy for use in a packing case factory at Grand Falls, New Brunswick.[30] With limited local supplies of fresh water and no ready place to store pulp logs, the mill produced only a small amount of pulp. Considered a "stock scheme" by local people, the company went into receivership in 1923. The principal merchants in Bear River were bankrupt. The wealth that Clarkes had carefully accumulated over decades from the town's old lumber and shipping trades had been lost in just a few years in a new industrial venture in which they had no previous experience. The failure of Clarkes had severely diminished the financial assets of the town, leaving it vulnerable to outside capital.

After an attempt by American investors to operate the mill failed, Lincoln Pulp Company, a subsidiary of Eastern Corporation of Brewer, Maine, bought the old Clarke forest land. New continental, corporate capital now controlled much of the pulpwood trade in Bear River. Lincoln employed some fifteen men in the area, mostly engaged in cutting pulpwood and loading it on vessels bound for Eastern's mill in Brewer (Plates 4–5). In the mid-1950s, lumberman John Henshaw reflected that "we might as well have nothing...all our raw material is shipped out of town" and "cutting pulp is no job for a 'white man.'" For local people, the collapse of the pulp mill "killed Bear River."[31] Today, the ruins of the mill stand as a forlorn memorial to the town's dreams of industry.

Besides the pulpwood land, outside capital took over several other businesses in Bear River. Among these was the town's electricity company. Established by Clarkes and other local businessmen, the electric light plant on the West Branch of the Bear River provided light to the local community during evenings and winter mornings. By 1927, the Annapolis Valley Electric Company, a subsidiary of an American holding company, Associated Gas & Electric, had bought the company.[32] The town's only bank also passed out of local control. The Commercial Bank of Windsor opened a branch in Bear River in 1898, and this was taken over by the Union Bank of Halifax in 1902. Eight years later, the Union Bank merged with the Royal Bank of Canada based in Montreal.[33] Between 1910 and the early 1920s, most of the key parts of the Bear River economy had passed out of the hands of local merchants and into those of corporations based in either Central Canada or the United States.[34] Decisions affecting the economy of Bear River were now made hundreds, if not thousands, of miles away by company officials who knew little, if anything, about the town.

After the collapse of the pulp venture, Bear River increasingly fell back on tourism. Instead of boosting itself as an emerging industrial metropolis, the town redefined itself as a picturesque retreat from the modern world.[35] Promotional publications referred to Bear River as the "Switzerland of Nova Scotia" (the river was the "Rhine of Nova Scotia") and "Cherry Town." In 1925, the Board of Trade distributed 5,000 booklets describing the natural scenery of the area to tourist agencies in Canada and the United States.[36] "Words cannot describe the varied loveliness of [Bear River's] valleys" wrote the author of *Historic Glimpses of Picturesque Bear River,* "nor the lofty grandeur of the towering hills crowned with well tilled farms or evergreen forests. In the many inlets formed by the windings of the river are shady little nooks, where an afternoon lunch and a book may be enjoyed." If picturesque scenery did not appeal, there was always the cherry festival, a mix of callithumpian parades, sports, and feasting. Some 3,000 to 5,000 tourists, many from Yarmouth, Digby, and Saint John, as well as from Lubec and Eastport in eastern Maine, attended the festival every July (Plate 6).[37]

The back country provided hunting and fishing for visiting sportsmen.[38] Affording "the finest trout fishing in Nova Scotia" and a "Hunter's Paradise," the lakes, streams, and woods attracted Americans from Boston and New York. Some of these sportsmen were rich businessmen, making an occasional foray into the Nova Scotian woods. Among them was John D. Rockefeller Jr., who passed through Bear River in October 1926, after hunting moose in Caledonia, Queens County.[39] Others were middle-class Americans, some with family ties in the area, who had summer homes in Bear River. Edgar McKay, for example, summered in town, and spent much of his time trout fishing in the back country.

Hunting and fishing gave considerable boost to the Bear River economy. Sportsmen needed provisions, camps, and guides. The Clarke Brothers store in Bear River advertised as the "Headquarters for Sportsmen's Supplies," and provided guides and outfits, with "birch bark and canvas canoes always on hand for sale."[40] Local guides built camps by lakes and streams. Wild Garden Sporting Camp on Sixth Lake Stream, owned by Les Rice, included a guides' cabin, two guest cabins, a well, and a cook house (Plate 7). The camp provided much of Rice's income from the middle 1930s.[41] Visiting sportsmen hired many local men as guides. Fire warden Carl Miller remembered "seeing as many as twenty-three guides with parties on Ninth Lake Stream at one time in those days [1920s]."[42] The guides were a mix of Bear River men and Micmacs from the reservation. Micmac Louis Harlow, for example, spent his summers guiding hunting and fishing parties from Milford House, about twelve miles east of Bear River. His wife, Madeline, made sweetgrass baskets for sale to tourists.[43]

Many Bear River guides took their skills to sportsmen's meets in Nova Scotia and the United States (Plate 8). Usually half the guides from the province who competed in the Boston Garden Hunting and Fishing Show were from Bear River. Among these guides was Eber Peck. After "ten days of exceptional feats of guides' lore and original wood craft stunts" at the Boston Garden show, Peck usually won the title of "Champion Woodsman of North America."[44] In 1947, Peck and three other guides from Bear River toured the United States, participating in sportsmen's shows in Boston, New York, Chicago, Buffalo, Des Moines, Los Angeles, Oakland, and San Diego.[45] Woods lore and skills, first learned in the lumber camps of Bear River, were now marketed in the major industrial cities of the continent. "Primitivism" appealed to urban sophisticates, who had lost touch with "nature" and yearned for a simpler and more manly life. With its guides sallying forth to win ever greater glories at sportsmen's shows and tourists flocking in for cherries, scenery, and hunting and fishing, Bear River was increasingly becoming a physical and psychological refuge from the modern industrial world.[46]

The power of the state was also suffusing through Bear River. With the outbreak of the First World War, the federal government began recruiting, raising war bonds, inspiring patriotic effort, and providing welfare in the community.[47] Many of the men from the western part of the province who joined the Nova Scotia Highlanders were from Bear River. By March 1916, the town had sent 120 recruits, the most in Annapolis County.[48] Although patriotism undoubtedly played an important part in this recruitment, such large numbers also reflected the lack of jobs in Bear River. On the home front, farmers and businessmen bought Victory Loan bonds to help finance the war effort, contributing $40,000 in the 1917 drive.[49] The federal government awarded National Badges of Honor to "Soldiers of the Soil," boys who worked on farms while the men were away fighting.[50] It also provided pensions to war widows.

After the war, the state's involvement increasingly turned to welfare. For many years, the federal government had responsibility for the Micmacs in Bear River, and this role expanded during the Great Depression to encompass other parts of the population. The national welfare program provided old-age pensions in 1934, unemployment insurance in 1940, and family allowances in 1944. Pensions helped many families in Bear River "to get along."[51] The federal government also provided jobs. The building of HMCS Cornwallis, the largest naval training station in the British Empire, at Deep Brook, six miles from Bear River in 1943-44 employed some 1,700 well-paid construction workers and a smaller number of regular maintenance staff (stenographers, bookkeepers, cooks, waitresses, carpenters, plumbers, electricians, firemen, grounds crew, etc.). In the mid-fifties, a quarter to a third of working people in Bear River had jobs at the base.

The provincial government also provided employment. In 1955, the province built a hydro dam on the East Branch of the Bear River, flooding one of the best trout streams in Nova Scotia. Sport fishing on the river, which had once attracted fishermen and employed local guides, gave way to the generation of electric power, much of it exported outside of Bear River. Maintaining the dam and power house employed a few men, and the province also hired men for road mending.[52] "When you get right down to it," declared the secretary of the Bear River Board of Trade, "pensions or government checks to the people who work for the Nova Scotia Power Commission or at the Naval Base [HMCS Cornwallis] keep this town alive."[53] In the mid-1950s, three-fourths of all expendable family income in Bear River derived directly or indirectly from government.[54]

With steady, if modest, incomes from government, those inhabitants of Bear River who formerly worked the land abandoned their fields to encroaching alders and pasture spruce. They "bought their living" in the form of canned goods from stores rather than raising farm-produce themselves. Many inhabitants purchased apples imported from California or New Zealand rather than pick Gravensteins and Pippins from their own disintegrating orchards. In the early 1950s, only a few cherries were still harvested, while the cherry festival was a shadow of its former self.[55]

By the First World War, cash increasingly circulated in the local economy, displacing old barter and credit arrangements. In 1915, Clarke Brothers started a "paydown system" and ended long-term credit.[56] Credit ties that formerly bound customers to merchants loosened, allowing people to shop beyond the town. At the same time, increasing use of automobiles permitted people to shop in Digby and Annapolis, while the national postal service facilitated the spread of mail-order. As early as 1906, the inhabitants of Bear River were clubbing together to send mail-orders to Eaton's and Simpson's in Ontario. "Every dollar sent away" wailed the *Digby Courier*, "goes to build up cities or towns hundreds of miles away, from which we can never hope to reap any benefits."[57] Although Clarkes brought out their own catalogue, "finely printed and beautifully illustrated," a few years later, they were far too small to compete against the giant mail-order houses in Toronto.[58] With the bankruptcy of Clarkes in 1926, the once-extensive dry goods business in Bear River closed.

Changes in employment also weakened the local retail sector. "Clarke Brothers used to hire a hundred men or more and they felt obligated to spend some of [their pay] in the store," observed Harold Davis in 1955. Many of these men had their wages credited in Clarkes' Bear River store. "Now people get their wages from the Base [CFB Cornwallis] or from pensions," continued Davis, "so they don't owe these store-keepers anything." As trade declined, storekeepers kept prices high to maintain profits. This inevitably led to more people shopping in Digby and Annapolis, where prices were lower.[59]

Modern communications and transportation also opened up the town. The first telephone line to Bear River was built in 1894, linking the town to the rest of the province.[60] By 1915, the line had extended to Victory, a back country settlement fourteen miles from town.[61] Seven years later, 166 subscribers in the Bear River area had telephones.[62] In June 1924, the office of Clarke Brothers put through a long-distance call to New York, the first from that part of Maritime Telephone and Telegraph Company's territory. New York was "heard as distinctively as though from Digby."[63] The town's

Fig. 9.   Geographic world of Bear River, c.1950.

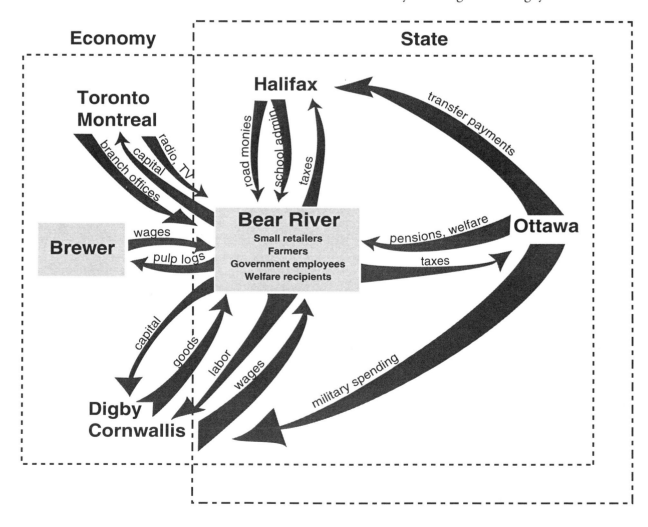

64

first radio receiver had appeared a year earlier, allowing people to "listen in" to urban popular culture.[64] Automobiles arrived in town in 1913 and were a common sight by the early 1920s. Yet it was not until the building of hard-top roads in the late 1940s that people began to drive from the town on a regular basis.[65] Many people commuted daily to the base at Deep Brook, or shopped for groceries in Digby. During the 1950s, Digby began to supplant Bear River as the local service center.

The change from a primary economy to a service economy and increasing reliance on jobs with well-defined working hours helped weaken people's ties to the natural environment and local time. The seasonal round of work no longer meant much to those inhabitants of Bear River who had abandoned farming and lumbering for jobs at the Naval Base and the Nova Scotia Power Corporation. For these people, clock-time, rather than natural time of tide and weather, measured workdays. Moreover, the switch from water to land transportation in the 1930s ended the town's dependence on the river; trucks and automobiles replaced schooners and the aging steamer *Bear River*. The natural world, once so important to work and life in Bear River, was now little more than a scenic backdrop.

By the early 1950s, Bear River had been transformed. The old mercantile economy had collapsed (Figure 9). Continental, corporate capital controlled many of the businesses of the old merchant families. Maritime trade had disappeared. Goods were no longer shipped by water to Saint John, Boston, or Havana. People and goods now traveled by rail, truck, or automobile. Instead of exporting produce, lumber, and piling to Boston, Bear River advertised for tourists from Central Canada and New England to visit the town. Many of these tourists fished in lakes and streams that once carried logs to mills; others admired the picturesque beauty of a town that once had shipyards, a sawmill, tanneries, and a river that once carried vessels loaded with lumber. The state, too, had enveloped the community by recruiting soldiers, giving out welfare, and providing jobs. Impersonal agreements between government bureaucrats and clients replaced the old paternalistic relationship between merchants and farmers. Modern communications, controlled not in Bear River or Digby but in New York and Toronto, carried urban culture into the living rooms of the community. Corporate and state power infiltrated the lives of Bear River people in a myriad of ways, replacing the old hierarchical relationship between town merchants and people. Although Bear River was still physically on the edge of Nova Scotia, new political and economic ties had turned it right around to face the interior of the continent.

Contours of Change 1890–1950

1. An end of an era. This dramatic
    photograph shows logs from
    diseased apple and cherry trees
    awaiting shipment at the Govern-
    ment Wharf, c.1921-1922. The logs
    were sold to a company operating in
    Annapolis, where they were turned
    into blocks for easy shipment to the
    United States.

2. An industrial vision for Bear River.
    This artist's drawing shows the
    Clarke Brothers kraft pulp mill at
    work, the Bluenose Express racing
    down the Dominion Atlantic Rail-
    way, and bustling wharves with
    steamships and sailing vessels.

C.P.R. & Victoria Bridges Mouth of Bear River, N.S.

3. The landscape of pulp, coal, and rail. The Bear River pulp mill, the Dominion Atlantic Railway, and the road bridge at the mouth of the Bear River, c.1919-1920. Compare this landscape of industry with that of farming, staple trade, and commerce in Plate 34.

4. Loading pulp logs on a vessel at the old Clarke Brothers wharf, Bear River village, c.1937-1939. Trucks have replaced the horses and oxen that once hauled sawn lumber to these wharves. (Historical Restoration Society of Annapolis County #971 Public Archives of Nova Scotia)

5. Schooner *Fred P. Elkin* being towed
    down river by the steamer *Bear River*
    c.1930-1931. The cargo of pulp
    wood was probably bound for
    Brewer, Maine.

6. The Bear River Pulp Company float
    in the Cherry Carnival Parade,
    c.1920. Awarded first prize, the
    float carries piping imported from
    Vancouver, BC, to be used for
    carrying water to the new pulp mill.
    Harold Davis stands with lead pair
    of oxen, owned by W.G. Clarke,
    while the teamster is Howard Yorke.

7. Wild Garden Sporting Camp
   owned by Les Rice on Sixth Lake
   Stream near Bear River, Summer
   1948. (Edgar McKay collection)

8. Start of four-man canoe race at the
   Nova Scotia Guides Association
   meet, Lake William, Lunenburg
   County, c.1937.

3

Conclusion

THE COLLAPSE of the traditional economy of semi-subsistence farming, commercial staple trade, and shipping in Bear River was repeated many times around the coasts of Maritime Canada during the late nineteenth and early twentieth centuries. A few outports, such as Liverpool on the South Shore of Nova Scotia and Bathurst on Chaleur Bay in New Brunswick, managed to make the transition from the old economy of wood, wind, and sail to the new one of pulp, coal, and rail, but many places failed. Weak resource bases, excessive distance from markets, and predatory external capital all hindered development. As economies weakened, people drifted away, farms were abandoned, old housing was not replaced, and stores and schools were closed. In some parts of Canada, the collapse of staple industries led to the complete abandonment of settlement, but in Bear River and other parts of rural Maritime Canada, limited farming, pulpwood cutting, tourism, and government employment and welfare tempered the end of the lumber trade. Nevertheless, in recent years, Bear River has lost its only bank, resident doctor, drugstore, and school. The closure of CFB Cornwallis, with the loss of 368 civilian jobs, was a further devastating blow.[1]

While much scholarship on the Maritimes has focused on the failure of places like Bear River to industrialize successfully, relatively little attention has been paid to other aspects of the modernization process. Here, the theoretical work of sociologist Anthony Giddens is suggestive. Giddens contends that modernization involves the rapid stretching of economic and political systems over time and space ("time-space distanciation") and an increasing trust in "abstract systems." In traditional, "class-divided societies," he argues, economic and political power was concentrated in the cities, the "power containers" of society, and tailed off into the countryside. When mercantile or state power extended into the countryside to trade, tax, or crush rebellion, its reach was often limited and episodic, because of the difficulties of overland transportation and communication, surveillance of people, and gathering of information. In Cole Harris's phrase, "town and countryside were different, if related, worlds."[2] Yet in modern, "class societies," improvements in transportation, methods of surveillance, and information storage allowed economic and political power to reach across much

Opposite: Automobiles take the lead in the Cherry Carnival, Bear River village, 1920. British flags still fly in front of the Grand Central House.

greater distances and infiltrate the lives of many more people. The nation-state, with its well-defined frontiers, replaced the walled city as the principal "power-container." As economic and political systems became stretched, interaction between people became less face-to-face and more between "absent others." This required placing trust in "expert systems" that increasingly managed the complex technologies and economies of modern society. Furthermore, replacement of barter by money facilitated exchange relations across time and space. No longer were exchanges limited to the actual physical transfer of goods. Taken together, improvements in transportation and communication, rise of expert systems, and greater and more rapid circulation of money acted as "disembedding mechanisms," lifting social and economic relations out of particular local contexts and stretching them over considerable time/space.[3] The "mooring lines" of life that helped tie people to familiar, local places became detached from their immediate physical surroundings and stretched to encompass much of the world.[4] What were distinct places with their own individual ways of life became increasingly "phantasmagoric" as they were thoroughly enmeshed and shaped by outside political and economic forces.[5]

The massive change that Giddens outlines took place in Europe over several hundred years. In Bear River and other parts of Maritime Canada the change is much less clearly defined.[6] From the beginning of the European encounter with northeastern North America, mercantile power was far more influential in shaping rural economies than Giddens suggests occurred in Europe. Although communication and trade were frequently slow and hazardous, the great dependence on water-transport allowed European merchants to establish a web of exchange relations that knitted staple producers in outports and trading posts in Maritime Canada to markets around the North Atlantic. The power of the state may have been less obvious in the eighteenth and early nineteenth centuries—for example, Crown land agents found it very difficult to implement government regulations in early nineteenth-century Cape Breton and New Brunswick[7]—but certainly by Confederation in 1867 provincial and federal governments were also reaching into the Maritime countryside. Provision of road monies, subsidies to transport, state education, censuses, and taxation all revealed the power of different levels of government. In spite of the considerable sway of mercantile and state power, however, places like Bear River were still relatively removed from the outside world. Slow overland transportation, dependence on natural resources, use of barter, and local control over the economy all helped sustain a sense of autonomy. Yet by the 1920s, many of the elements that characterize Giddens's modern, "class societies" were making themselves felt in Bear River. The growing influence of the state, takeover of key parts of the economy by corporate capital, trust in outside financial and engineering "experts" who advised the Bear River Pulp Company, circulation of money, and greater personal mobility all helped break down Bear River's relative isolation and integrate it into the national space. The tight web of economic and personal connections that formerly bound people to place was dramatically loosened. While the inhabitants of Bear River at the beginning of the twentieth century still felt they controlled their collective destiny, this was not the case fifty years later. By then, they had left behind their sailing ships, horses, and oxen and climbed aboard the "careering juggernaut" of modernity.[8]

Maritime writer Ernest Buckler caught something of this perspective in his work.[9] Writing not twenty-five miles from Bear River at Centerlea in the heart of the Annapolis Valley, Buckler focused on the transformation of the traditional rural world that he knew as a boy. Much of his writing celebrated continuity between people and place, humans and nature, past and present. "We own ourselves completely" he declared in *Ox Bells and Fireflies,* "everything around us seems to be the fruit of us." "You walked down the road and it took the imprint of your footsteps. The field that bordered the road was all yours to the depths of the earth." The landscape was familiar and personalized: "The 'Bart Ramsay place' would always be the 'Bart Ramsay place,' however often it changed hands. The sharp twist in the road near Davy Langille's house would always be 'Davy's Bend.'" For Buckler, the lower Annapolis Valley, between Bridgetown and Digby, was the "greenest island of all."[10] Yet in *The Mountain and the Valley,* the modern urban-industrial world pressed in. "The road was paved now. There were cars and radios. A bus line passed the door. There was a railway along the river. With this grafting from the outside world, the place itself seemed older; as the old who are not remembered are old." City fashions influenced local speech and dress; foreign corporate capital transformed the old agrarian landscape: "a big American company [most likely Eastern Corporation] had bought these farms solely for their timber. The company had no interest in the houses or the fields. The people had moved to town."[11] The outside world had eventually enveloped Buckler's greenest island, much as it had Ed McKay's childhood home.

Today, Bear River, like the rest of Maritime Canada, is exposed to forces well beyond the confines of the Canadian nation-state. The nexus of government welfare and tourism that served for forty or fifty years as panaceas for places like Bear River has been radically changed. Growing government debt, much of it held by foreign investors, has led to reduced federal transfer payments to the Maritimes and slashing of provincial budgets. Overseas bondholders, rather than politicians in Ottawa and Halifax, increasingly call the tune. Free trade between Canada and the United States threatens to replace the old east-west economic framework of the National Policy with renewed north-south links. Capital and commodities flow back and forth across the border but people with few or no skills are refused. Unlike the early twentieth century, the "Boston States" are out of reach for Nova Scotia's unemployed. Tourism, too, has changed. The building of a Dutch windmill on the old Clarke wharves by recent immigrants from the Netherlands, the "Disneyfication" of Nova Scotia history in the nearby Upper Clements theme park, and, farther afield, the thousands of Japanese tourists who swarm over Anne of Green Gables cottage on Prince Edward Island each summer testify to the globalization of tourism and the fragmentation of the past. The old continuities between past and present that existed in Bear River and many other places in the Maritimes no longer hold. A Dutch windmill cheek-by-jowl with Yankee-influenced classical revival architecture does not appear incongruous to tourists who have little sense of past times and places. The "mooring lines" of life have indeed been stretched. For better or for worse, Bear River is caught up in a global world that will dramatically rearrange the warp and weft of life and work in the town in ways still to be seen.

Notes

Preface

1. Ian McKay (ed.), *The Challenge of Modernity: A Reader on Post-Confederation Canada* (Toronto: McGraw-Hill Ryerson, 1992); Donald Kerr and Deryck W. Holdsworth (eds.), *Historical Atlas of Canada Volume III: Addressing the Twentieth Century* (Toronto: University of Toronto Press, 1990).

2. John Herd Thompson, 'Writing About Rural Life and Agriculture' in *Writing About Canada* ed. John Schultz, 97-119. (Scarborough, Ont.: Prentice-Hall Canada, 1990).

3. For an important recent collection of essays on the transformation of the rural Maritimes, see Daniel Samson (ed.), *Contested Countryside: Rural Workers and Modern Society in Atlantic Canada, 1800-1950* (Fredericton, NB: Acadiensis Press, 1994).

4. Known as the "Stirling County Study of Psychiatric Disorder and Sociocultural Environment," this research was published in Charles C. Hughes *et al., People of Cove and Woodlot: Communities from the Viewpoint of Social Psychiatry* (New York: Basic Books, 1960).

5. Hughes, *People of Cove and Woodlot,* 22-23.

6. E. Foster Hall, *Heritage Remembered: The Story of Bear River* (Bear River, NS: Bear River New Horizons' Centre, 1981).

7. Advertisement in Lennie D. Wade, *Historic Glimpses of Picturesque Bear River* (n.d.).

8. Wade, *Historic Glimpses.*

9. Graeme Wynn, '"Images of the Acadian Valley": The Photographs of Amos Lawson Hardy,' *Acadiensis* 15, 1 (Autumn 1985): 59-83.

10. Edgar McKay, 'Bear River, NS — Summer, 1954: Random Impressions and Observations of Edgar B. McKay,' typescript, 2-4.

11. For the photographs by Pratsch, see Robert A. Weinstein, *Grays Harbor 1885-1913* (Harmondsworth: Penguin Books, 1978).

Introduction

1. R. Cole Harris, 'The Pattern of Early Canada,' in *People, Places, Patterns, Processes: Geographical Perspectives on the Canadian Past* ed. Graeme Wynn, 358-373. (Toronto: Copp Clark Pitman, 1990). See also R. Cole Harris (ed.), *Historical Atlas of Canada Volume I: From the Beginning to 1800* (Toronto: University of Toronto Press, 1987); Kerr and Holdsworth, *Historical Atlas of Canada,* and Graeme Wynn, 'Forging a Canadian Nation,' in *North America: The Historical Geography of a Changing Continent* eds. Robert D. Mitchell and Paul A. Groves, 373-409. (Totowa, NJ: Rowman & Littlefield, 1987).

2. Anthony Giddens, *The Consequences of Modernity* (Stanford: Stanford University Press, 1990), especially 17-21.

3. For a superb survey of these changes, see Graeme Wynn, 'The Maritimes: the Geography of Fragmentation and Underdevelopment,' in *Heartland and Hinterland: A Geography of Canada* ed. L.D. McCann, 157-213. (Scarborough, ONT: Prentice-Hall Canada, 1982). See also the various essays in E.R. Forbes and D.A. Muise (eds.), *The Atlantic Provinces in Confederation* (Toronto: University of Toronto Press, 1993).

4. The classic statement of this transition is T.W. Acheson, 'The National Policy and the Industrialization of the Maritimes, 1880-1910,' *Acadiensis* 1, 2 (Spring 1972): 3-28.

5. L.D. McCann, 'Metropolitanism and Branch Businesses in the Maritimes, 1881-1931,' *Acadiensis* 13, 1 (Autumn 1983): 112-125; and Kris E. Inwood, 'Maritime Industrialization from 1870 to 1910: A Review of the Evidence and Its Interpretation,' *Acadiensis* 21, 1 (Autumn 1991): 132-155.

6. L.D. McCann, 'Shock Waves in the Old Economy: The Maritime Urban System during the Great Transformation c.1867-1939,' in *Shock Waves: The Maritime Urban System in the New Economy* eds. George J. De Benedetti and Rodolphe H. Lamarche, 9-42. (Moncton, NB: Canadian Institute for Research on Regional Development, 1994).

Chapter One

1. Bear River comprises the townships of Bear River in Annapolis County and Hillsburgh in Digby County. For the early settlement of Hillsburgh, see Isaiah W. Wilson, *A Geography and History of the County of Digby, Nova Scotia* (Halifax, NS: Holloway, 1900, reprinted by Mika 1972), especially 171-172.

2. Edgar McKay interview with Harold Davis, 20 August 1955.

3. Wynn, 'The Maritimes'; Stephen J. Hornsby, *Nineteenth-Century Cape Breton: A Historical Geography* (Montreal and Kingston: McGill-Queen's University Press, 1992).

4. *Census of Canada, 1891.*

5. McKay interview with Davis, 21 July 1955.

6. McKay interview with Herb Hazelton, 21 July 1955.

7. McKay interview with John Morine, 21 July 1955.

8. Because of the lack of a nominal agricultural census for the closing years of the nineteenth century, this discussion of the agricultural economy of Bear River is necessarily impressionistic. It is clear, though, that agriculture in Bear River straddled both the lumbering and farming zones identified in Robert MacKinnon and Graeme Wynn, 'Nova Scotian Agriculture in the "Golden Age": A New Look,' in *Geographical Perspectives on the Maritime Provinces* ed. D. Day, 47-60. (Halifax: St. Mary's University Press, 1988).

9. McKay, 'Some brief notes on the economic history of Bear River,' typescript, 2.

10. *Digby Courier* 15 November 1895.

11. McKay commentary on Harris photographs.

12. McKay interview with Davis, 21 July 1955.

13. For another regional example of farming in an 'urban shadow,' see Robert MacKinnon, 'Farming the Rock: The Evolution of Commercial Agriculture around St. John's, Newfoundland, to 1945,' *Acadiensis* 20, 2 (Spring 1991): 32-85.

14. McKay commentary on Harris photographs.

15. *Digby Courier* 22 July 1898.

16. For development of the apple industry in neighboring Annapolis Valley, see Margaret Conrad, 'Apple Blossom Time in the Annapolis Valley, 1880-1957,' *Acadiensis* 9, 2 (Spring 1980) 14-39.

17. McKay interview with Morine, 21 July 1955.

18. McKay, 'Economic history of Bear River,' 2.

19. *Telephone* 17 April 1901.

20. *Digby Courier* for 30 March 1917 records shipments of turnips to Boston via Saint John.

21. McKay interview with Alpheus Marshall, 25 August 1954.

22. McKay interview with Marshall, 25 August 1954.

23. *Digby Courier* 10 January 1902, 15 January 1904.

24. McKay interviews with John Henshaw, 3 and 9 August 1954 and Roy Miller, 20 July 1955; *Digby Courier* 17 June 1892, 22 February 1895, 18 October 1895, 22 May 1896. David C. Smith discusses the development of markets in lumber for shipbuilding and in hemlock bark for tanning in *A History of Lumbering in Maine, 1861-1960* (Orono, ME: University of Maine Press, 1972), 214-220.

25. The multiple interests of Clarke Brothers were typical of many merchants in the Maritimes. For a similar firm, see the discussion of the Campbell family at Weymouth, close to Bear River, in L.D. McCann, '"Living A Double Life": Town and Country in the Industrialization of the Maritimes,' in *Geographical Perspectives* ed. Day, 93-113.

26. *Digby Courier* 19 September 1902.

27. *Digby Courier* 25 December 1903.

28. McKay interview with Henshaw, 9 August 1954.

29. Such occupational pluralism was typical in the Maritimes. See, for example, Rusty Bitterman, 'Farm Households and Wage Labour in the Northeastern Maritimes in the Early 19th Century,' *Labour/Le Travail* 31 (1993): 13-45; Hornsby, *Nineteenth-Century Cape Breton* 72-73, 140-42; McCann, 'Living A Double Life'; and Graeme Wynn, *Timber Colony: A Historical Geography of Early Nineteenth Century New Brunswick* (Toronto: University of Toronto Press, 1981), 72-86.

30. McKay interview with Henshaw, 9 August 1954.

31. *Digby Courier* 16 October 1891, *Bear River News* 20 March 1909.

32. McKay interview with Henshaw, 3 August 1954.

33. McKay interview with Henshaw, 3 August 1954. For a discussion of similar lumbering practices in a neighboring area, see James Morrison and Lawrence Friend, *"We Have Held Our Own": The Western Interior of Nova Scotia, 1800-1940* (Ottawa: National Historic Parks and Sites Branch Parks Canada, 1981), 43-50.

34. "Clarke & Miller start a big drive at Lake Franklin for the Lake Jolly mill this week." *Digby Courier* 20 March 1903.

35. McKay commentary on Harris photograph.

36. McKay interview with Henshaw, 3 August 1954.

37. McKay interview with Miller, 20 July 1955.

38. McKay interview with Henshaw, 9 August 1954, and Walter Brown, 11 August 1954.

39. McKay interview with Reginald Benson, 4 February 1955.

40. McKay interview with Reginald Benson, 4 February 1955. For background on these changes, see Eric W. Sager with Gerald E. Panting, *Maritime Capital: The Shipping Industry in Atlantic Canada 1820-1914* (Montreal and Kingston: McGill-Queen's University Press, 1990), 54-60.

41. McKay interview with Maurice Benson, 3 September 1954.

42. McKay interview with Reginald Benson, 4 February 1955.

43. McKay interview with Reginald Benson, 4 February 1955. The towing of "hard pine sticks" across the Bay of Fundy for use as masts on a Clarke Brothers schooner is recorded in the *Digby Courier* 19 April 1901.

44. McKay interview with Maurice Benson, 3 September 1954.

45. McKay interview with Reginald Benson, 4 February 1955.

46. McKay interview with Maurice Benson, 3 September 1954.

47. McKay interview with Marshall, 25 August 1954.

48. For a useful study of shipbuilding elsewhere in the Fundy area, see A. Gregg Finley, 'The Morans of St. Martins, N.B., 1850-1880: Toward an Understanding of Family Participation in Maritime Enterprise,' in *The Enterprising Canadians: Entrepreneurs and Economic Development in Eastern Canada,* eds. Lewis R. Fischer and Eric W. Sager, 37-54. (St. John's: Memorial University, 1979).

49. McKay interview with Reginald Benson, 4 February 1955.

50. McKay interview with Marshall, 25 August 1954.

51. *Digby Courier* 21 September 1900.

52. McKay interview with Carl Miller, 11 August 1954.

53. McKay interview with Roy Miller, 20 July 1955.

54. McKay interview with Carl Miller, 11 August 1954.

55. *Digby Courier* 10 April 1891. This migration from Bear River was repeated throughout the Maritimes. For other examples, see Hornsby, *Nineteenth-Century Cape Breton* 186-200.

56. *Digby Courier* 4 April 1902, 20 March 1903, 14 April 1905; McKay interview with Henshaw, 9 August 1954.

57. McKay interview with Henshaw, 9 August 1954.

58. *Digby Courier* 8 April, 6 May 1904.

59. McKay interview with Henshaw, 3 August 1954. For the migration of Nova Scotians to Boston, see Alan A. Brookes (ed.), '"The Provincials" by Albert Kennedy,' *Acadiensis* 4, 2 (1975): 85-101.

60. *Digby Courier* 14 August 1908; *Bear River News* 5 August 1911. For "harvest specials," see John H. Thompson, 'Bringing in the Sheaves: The Harvest Excursionists, 1890-1929,' *Canadian Historical Review* 59, 4 (1978): 467-89.

61. Betsy Beattie, '"Going Up to Lynn": Single, Maritime-Born Women in Lynn, Massachusetts, 1879-1930,' *Acadiensis* 14, 1 (Autumn 1992): 65-86.

62. McKay interview with Enoch Peck, 28 August 1954.

63. Mary E. Beattie, 'Obligation and Opportunity: Single Maritime Women in Boston, 1870 to 1930.' Unpublished Ph.D. dissertation, University of Maine, 1994, 45-47; and information supplied by Edgar McKay.

64. McKay interview with Marshall, 25 August 1954.

65. McKay interview with Reginald Benson, 4 February 1955.

66. *Digby Courier* 7 January 1921.

67. *Digby Courier* 25 April 1902, 24 March 1905, 15 May 1908.

68. McKay interview with Marshall, Summer 1955.

69. McKay, 'Saturday Night at the Bridge,' typescript, 20 August 1955, 3.

70. *Bear River News* 7 July 1908.

71. Based on weekly dates of travel listed in the "Local and Personal" columns of the Bear River *Telephone* 1900-1902. The number of issues of the *Telephone* each month may have affected the monthly totals. For the three years (1900, 1901, 1902), only nine issues survive for March, whereas fifteen issues are extant for January and October and fourteen issues for May. All other months have between eleven and thirteen issues. Although the March total may be too low, the total for February is based on all twelve issues published for that month over three years.

72. *Digby Courier* 22 December 1933.

73. Ernest Buckler, *Ox Bells and Fireflies* (New York: Alfred A. Knopf, 1968) 89.

74. For the importance of local environmental knowledge in other parts of Atlantic Canada, see John J. Mannion, *Point Lance in Transition: The Transformation of a Newfoundland Outport* (Toronto: McClelland and Stewart, 1976), and Gerald L. Pocius, *A Place to Belong: Community and Everyday Space in Calvert, Newfoundland* (Montreal and Kingston: McGill-Queen's University Press, 1991). For a study of a community in Nova Scotia somewhat similar to Bear River, see Eric Ross, 'The Rise and Fall of Pictou Island,' in *Studies of Small Town Life in the Maritimes* ed. Larry McCann, 161-188. (Fredericton, NB: Acadiensis Press, 1987).

75. R.A. Lewis to Bear River Steamship Co., 19 July 1906, Clarke Papers, MG 3/3201 Public Archives of Nova Scotia.

76. Graeme Wynn, 'A Province Too Much Dependent on New England,' *Canadian Geographer* 31, 2 (1987): 98-113, 'A Region of Scattered Settlements and Bounded Possibilities: Northeastern America 1775-1800,' *Canadian Geographer* 31, 4 (1987): 319-338, and 'New England's Outpost in the Nineteenth Century,' in *The Northeastern Borderlands: Four Centuries of Interaction* eds. Stephen J. Hornsby, Victor A. Konrad, and James J. Herlan, 64-90. (Fredericton, NB: Acadiensis Press, 1989).

77. Peter Ennals and Deryck Holdsworth, 'The Cultural Landscape of the Maritime Provinces,' in *Geographical Perspectives* ed. by Day, 1-14.

78. *Telephone* 30 January, 6 February 1901.

79. The importance of the Bay of Fundy axis is stressed in Carmen Miller, 'The Restoration of Greater Nova Scotia,' in *Canada and the Burden of Unity* ed. David Jay Bercuson, 44-59. (Toronto: Macmillan, 1977).

80. This approximate figure is derived from linking the data in the newspaper to Dun & Bradstreet records and the nominal census of 1901.

81. Alan A. Brookes, 'The Golden Age and the Exodus: The Case of Canning, Kings County,' *Acadiensis* 11, 1 (Autumn 1981): 57-82.

82. Brookes, 'Golden Age and the Exodus,' 78.

83. The demographer E.G. Ravenstein noted the pattern of short-distance female migration in nineteenth-century Britain, and it has been confirmed in many empirical studies. For the Maritimes, see Beattie, '"Going Up to Lynn,"' and Hornsby, *Nineteenth-Century Cape Breton,* 195.

84. Wynn, 'The Maritimes.'

Chapter Two

1. McKay, 'Random Impressions and Observations,' typescript, Summer 1954.

2. This decline, particularly after 1891, follows the province-wide pattern. See the discussion of demographic change in Robert MacKinnon, 'Agriculture and Rural Change in Nova Scotia, 1851-1951,' unpublished mss.

3. *Dun & Bradstreet Reference Book* 1900, 1910, 1920, 1930, 1940, and 1950.

4. For out-migration from the Maritime provinces at this time, see Patricia A. Thornton, 'The Problem of Out-Migration from Atlantic Canada, 1871-1921: A New Look,' *Acadiensis* 15, 1 (1985): 3-34, and for a slightly earlier period, see Alan A. Brooks, 'Out-Migration from the Maritime Provinces,

1860-1900: Some Preliminary Considerations,' *Acadiensis* 5, 2 (1976): 26-55.

5. *Census of Canada, 1941*

6. McKay interview with Miller, 11 August 1954.

7. McKay interview with Henshaw, 3 August 1954.

8. MacKinnon, 'Agriculture and Rural Change.'

9. *Digby Courier* 7 January 1921.

10. *Digby Courier* 10 June 1904.

11. *Digby Courier* 16 June 1922, 11 May 1923, 23 May 1924, 20 May 1933.

12. *Digby Courier* 6 December 1945, 14 November 1946.

13. *Digby Courier* 14 June, 20 September 1901.

14. *Digby Courier* 16 January 1925. For the general context, see Sager and Panting, *Maritime Capital.*

15. *Digby Courier* 31 August 1906.

16. *Digby Courier* 25 October 1912.

17. *Digby Courier* 25 January 1935.

18. *Digby Courier* 25 March 1943.

19. Attempts by merchants in the Maritimes to invest in the new industrial economy are well documented, particularly in Acheson, 'National Policy'; Catherine A. Johnson, 'The Search for Industry in Newcastle, New Brunswick, 1899-1914,' *Acadiensis* 13, 1 (Autumn 1983): 93-111; and in L.D. McCann, 'Staples and the New Industrialism in the Growth of Post-Confederation Halifax,' *Acadiensis* 8, 2 (Spring 1979): 47-79, 'The Mercantile-Industrial Transition in the Metal Towns of Pictou County, 1857-1931,' *Acadiensis* 10, 2 (Spring 1981): 29-64, and 'Industrialization and the Maritimes' in *Historical Atlas of Canada* eds. Kerr and Holdsworth, pl. 24.

20. *Digby Courier* 4 March 1904, 14 July 1905, 2 February 1906, 1 February 1907, 28 April 1911, 24 January 1913, 19 May 1916. For the larger context of railway building in the region, see Shirley E. Woods, *Cinder & Saltwater: The Story of Atlantic Canada's Railways* (Halifax: Nimbus, 1992).

21. For the spread of the pulp industry in neighboring New Brunswick, see Kerr and Holdsworth, *Historical Atlas of Canada,* pl. 24; and Bill Parenteau, 'The Woods Transformed: The Emergence of the Pulp and Paper Industry in New Brunswick, 1918-1931,' *Acadiensis* 22, 1 (Autumn 1992): 5-43.

22. *Digby Courier* 16 September 1904. For background on the Sissiboo Pulp & Paper Company, see McCann, '"Living a double life,"' 100-103.

23. *Digby Courier* 29 March 1912.

24. *Digby Courier* 21, 28 March 1913.

25. *Digby Courier* 28 March 1919.

26. *Digby Courier* 30 May 1919, 31 December 1920.

27. *Digby Courier* 20 May 1921.

28. *Digby Courier* 2 September, 23 December 1921, 30 March 1923.

29. *Digby Courier* 12 November 1920.

30. *Digby Courier* 19 November 1920.

31. McKay interview with Henshaw, 9 August 1954.

32. *Digby Courier* 27 April 1928, and information supplied by Ed McKay.

33. *Digby Courier* 7 January 1921. See also Kerr and Holdsworth, *Historical Atlas of Canada* pl. 9.

34. For the general context, see McCann, 'Metropolitanism'; and Wynn, 'New England's Outpost.'

35. Wade, *Historic Glimpses.*

36. For a promotional story on the scenic charms of Bear River, "this pocket edition of Paradise," aimed at the urban market, see 'Bear River As Seen by the Suburban Representative,' *The Suburban,* 22 September 1906.

37. *Digby Courier* 27 July 1923, 22 July 1938.

38. For hunting in Kejimkujik National Park, see Morrison and Friend, "*We Have Held Our Own*", 84-99; for guiding in Nova Scotia, see Mike Parker, *Guides of the North Woods: Hunting and Fishing Tales from Nova Scotia 1860-1960* (Halifax, NS: Nimbus, 1990); and for American tourists in Nova Scotia, see James H. Morrison, 'American Tourism in Nova Scotia, 1871-1940,' *Nova Scotia Historical Review* 2, 2 (1982): 40-51.

39. *Digby Courier* 15 October 1926.

40. Wade, *Historic Glimpses.*

41. Parker, *Guides,* 74-78; McKay interview with Leslie Rice, 10 September 1954.

42. McKay interview with Carl Miller, 11 August 1954.

43. McKay, 'Some Random Comments by and about Louis Harlow, Micmac Indian,' summers 1954-1955.

44. *Digby Courier* 27 April 1934, 3 May 1935; Parker, *Guides,* 175-176.

45. *Digby Courier* 29 May 1947.

46. For the general background of the wilderness cult, see Roderick Nash, *Wilderness and the American Mind* (New Haven: Yale, 1967), especially 141-160. The theme of anti-modernism and the rise of tourism in Nova Scotia is brilliantly dealt with in Ian McKay, *The Quest of the Folk* (Montreal and Kingston: McGill-Queen's University Press, 1994), although McKay says little about the cult of the wilderness.

47. For the general context, see Kerr and Holdsworth, *Historical Atlas of Canada,* pl. 26.

48. *Digby Courier* 3 March 1916.

49. *Digby Courier* 30 November 1917.

50. *Digby Courier* 23 August 1918.

51. The arrival of the first old-age pensions was noted in the *Digby Courier* 6 April 1934. The quotation is from McKay, 'Economic History,' 5.

52. *Digby Courier* 30 December 1921.

53. McKay interview with Clayton M. Harris, Secretary of the Bear River Board of Trade, 14 July 1955.

54. McKay, 'Economic History,' 4-5.

55. McKay, 'Economic History.'

56. *Digby Courier* 8 January 1915.

57. *Digby Courier* 20 March 1923.

58. *Digby Courier* 16 March 1906.

59. McKay interview with Davis, 20 August 1955.

60. *Digby Courier* 20 July 1894.

61. *Digby Courier* 10 December 1915.

62. *Digby Courier* 14 April 1922.

63. *Digby Courier* 24 June 1921.

64. *Digby Courier* 20 March 1923.

65. For the building of roads, see *Digby Courier* 7 June 1945, 6 February 1947, 29 January 1948.

Chapter Three

1. *Maclean's* 7 March 1994.

2. Cole Harris, 'Power, Modernity, and Historical Geography,' *Annals of the Association of American Geographers* 81, 4 (1991): 671-683.

3. This abbreviated discussion of Giddens's complex ideas on "time-space distanciation" is drawn from *A Contemporary Critique of Historical Materialism* (Berkeley: University of California Press, 1981), 90-108, 157-81; *The Nation-State and Violence* (Berkeley and Los Angeles: University of California Press, 1987); and *Consequences of Modernity*.

4. The metaphor of "mooring lines" comes from Derek Gregory's fine discussion of Giddens in *Geographical Imaginations* (Oxford: Basil Blackwell, 1994), 118.

5. Giddens, *Consequences of Modernity*, 19.

6. G. Wynn, 'Ideology, Society, and State in the Maritime Colonies of British North America, 1840-1860,' in *Colonial Leviathan: State Formation in Mid-Nineteenth-Century Canada* eds. Allan Greer and Ian Radforth, 284-328. (Toronto: University of Toronto Press, 1992).

7. Hornsby, *Nineteenth-Century Cape Breton*, 54-56; and G. Wynn, 'Administration in Adversity: The Deputy Surveyors and Control of New Brunswick Crown Forest Before 1844,' *Acadiensis* 7, 1 (Autumn 1977): 49-65.

8. Giddens, *Consequences of Modernity* 53.

9. This connection, suggested by Graeme Wynn, is more fully explored in Erik Kristiansen, 'Time, Memory, and Rural Transformation: Rereading History in the Fiction of Charles Bruce and Ernest Buckler,' in *Contested Countryside* ed. Samson, 225-256.

10. Buckler, *Ox Bells,* 36, 86, 88, 83.

11. Ernest Buckler, *The Mountain and the Valley* (Toronto: McClelland and Stewart, 1970 ed.), 229, 253.